The Fall of the House of
MURDAUGH

Moonshine, Manipulation and Murder in South Carolina

by Michael M. DeWitt Jr.

Published by

Evening Post Books
Charleston, South Carolina

Copyright © 2024 Michael DeWitt Jr.
All rights reserved.
First edition

Author: Michael DeWitt Jr.
Editor: John M. Burbage
Designer: Gill Guerry

First printing 2024
Printed in the United States of America

A CIP catalog record for this book has been applied
for from the Library of Congress.

ISBN: 978-1-929647-92-7

Dedicated to the fine folks of

Hampton County, S.C.,

especially those victimized by

Alex Murdaugh.

CONTENTS

ACKNOWLEDGMENTS

Thanks to the seasoned Gannett journalists who supported me in telling this extraordinary story of family privilege, politics, greed and murder in the Lowcountry of rural South Carolina. A special acknowledgement to Carol Motsinger for helping me find my way as a nonfiction writer while aiding greatly with research and encouragement. Many thanks to my wife and children for their sacrifices while their loved one went missing among forgotten files of history and inside the crowded Colleton County Courthouse in search of truth.

And, finally, a sincere Southern "Thank you kindly!" to Evening Post Books of Charleston, S.C., and my editor, John M. Burbage, who along with Managing Editor Elizabeth Hollerith, Assistant Managing Editor Alex Lanning, graphic artist Gill Guerry and indexer Kathryn Smith are the best book-publishing team in the business.

INTRODUCTION

HAMPTON, S.C. —

I did not have to go far to find this story. The Murdaugh family murders hit home like a rogue tornado. As a native son of this swampy, out-of-the-way place near the coast of lower South Carolina, I was hesitant to share what I knew about the characters in this chronicle of privilege, greed, wealth and ruin. However, as the editor and sole reporter of the venerable *Hampton County Guardian* weekly newspaper, there was no time to muse on it. I had a job to do.

For eight years and counting I have reported the torrent of twists and turns in the destruction of Randolph Murdaugh Sr.'s powerful, largely self-serving, South Carolina legal dynasty, and pieces of the wreckage continue to fall all around.

There are few heroes in this century-old saga of the Murdaugh law firm's founding father and his lawyer progeny. The ultimate villain is Randolph Sr.'s great-grandson, Alex Murdaugh, recently judged entirely evil and given two life sentences without parole in state prison for murdering his wife and youngest son. As I write these words in the fall of 2023 the narrative continues: A re-trial of Alex for gunning down his loved ones is possible based on unresolved jury tampering allegations about the Colleton County clerk of court before, during and after the jury's deliberations. Are they true? How long will it take to find out? Does it matter?

Fact is, Alex won't be freed any time soon, if ever. He is currently imprisoned in relative isolation in a South Carolina maximum-security facility for killing his wife and son. Being a lifer in the S.C. penal system is a dangerous, difficult predicament — especially for a corrupt ex-lawyer/prosecutor named Murdaugh. However, he has already pleaded guilty to federal and state financial-fraud charges with sentences worth 750 years. If he triumphs in a retrial on his state murder convictions, Alex might seek to spend the rest of his life somewhat safer and perhaps more comfortable in the federal penitentiary system.

Still, the House of Murdaugh has fallen after more than a century. Its history alternately sparked and smoldered through the years as one lawyer named Randolph after another passed the mantle from scion to scion for four generations until the early morning darkness of Feb. 24, 2019, when a boating accident stole the life of a local girl out partying. Alex Murdaugh's youngest son, Paul, was with friends when his father's boat crashed in the fog that engulfed the bridge over Archers Creek, near Beaufort, and the investigation of who was driving at that moment was suspect from the start. It dragged on until June 7, 2021 when the bloody bodies of Paul Murdaugh, 22, and his mother, Maggie Murdaugh, 52, were reported on a 911 call by Alex at the kennels of the family's 1,700-acre hunting retreat in Colleton County. Mother and son had been executed — Maggie with several rounds from a semi-automatic rifle, and Paul with two blasts from a 12-gauge shotgun.

Who would do such a thing, and why?

The Randolph Murdaugh family emerged in the early 1900s to become a homegrown legal and political dynasty that capitalized on dealing out justice with one hand and raking in fees awarded for personal injuries with the other. By the time of the murders more than a century later, the family narrative was so deeply layered that only a few insiders could sort out the truth. I am one of those insiders.

This account is the truth based on all I know thus far about this remarkable family. It details the rise to power of Randolph Murdaugh Sr. (born 1887; died 1940) and three subsequent generations of preening male descendants of the same name who maintained the family's lucrative law firm until it collapsed in disgrace in 2023.

For the most part, I avoid hearsay in telling the tale. But the small-town rumor mill did play a role in unraveling the Murdaugh mystique. At times the story reads like a crime novel, but what unfolds is real and riveting — an account of the steady rise of a prominent Southern family and the cold-blooded murders that brought it down. The focus is on talented, troublesome Murdaugh men and how their privileged lives played out as they manipulated South Carolina's long-enduring, incestuous nature of misplaced pride, errant homegrown politics and amoral social prominence. The book is based on legal documents, local histories, newspaper articles, and innumerable conversations with people who thought they knew the family well — including Alex Murdaugh's financial victims who did not know until it was too late.

Please note mention herein of "the Murdaughs" or "the Murdaugh family" refers only to those connected to founder Randolph Murdaugh Sr.'s evolving law firm and South Carolina's 14th Judicial Circuit Solicitor's Office. There are numerous other Murdaughs in the Lowcountry.

So join me on a saga that began in 1865 near the end of the Confederacy and concludes 158 years later with a guilty verdict in the double-murder trial of a narcissistic father accused of executing his wife and youngest son in a desperate attempt to preserve himself as well as his family name. It's a tragedy with no main hero, a drama yet to completely unfold, and a narrative sure to captivate all who care to read it.

Prologue: Come fly with me

A fat, black fly hones in on what's left of a chicken wing on the sidewalk in front of Regional Finance Co., one of six micro-loan shops on Lee Avenue, Hampton, a small town in a rural county of the same name deep in South Carolina's lower coastal region. The street, which honors Confederate Gen. Robert E. Lee, runs from the railroad tracks to the county courthouse, dedicated in honor of another Confederate general, Wade Hampton III, a wealthy Southern Democrat elected governor in 1876. Federal troops left following his election after 15 years of post-war occupation of South Carolina known as Reconstruction. The town and newly formed county were named in honor of Gov. Hampton, who laid the cornerstone of the courthouse.

The building faces Lee Avenue, only three blocks long and bounded on the north by CSX railroad tracks, which stretch southwest from branch headquarters near Yemassee across the Savannah River to Augusta, Ga. The locals rarely refer to the street as Lee Avenue anymore; it's simply "main street" now. Economic-development bureaucrats have renovated offices next door to shuttered Vincent's Drug Store. A sign on Lee Avenue proclaims Hampton a "Historic Downtown," although most of main street's businesses are boarded up, crumbling or leveled. Roughly half of the real estate on the avenue is empty lots. It's a street of contrasts, a snapshot of small-town America where a false sense of refinement and riches rubs elbows with the reality of rubble and ruin.

Hampton was founded in 1878 as a "white county," an inland solace 40-odd miles away from the old port town of Beaufort with its Yankee carpetbaggers and uneducated free blacks, to quote a local history titled *Both Sides of the Swamp*. But the joke is on Hampton's founding fathers: of the county's roughly 19,000 documented residents today, slightly more than half are people of color, most of them descendants of enslaved Africans. All the while, the county's total population steadily dwindled after Gov. Hampton laid the stone at the courthouse square. More than 3,000 souls have abandoned this place since the last U.S. Census — a trend not likely to reverse itself anytime soon, if ever.

Well-paying jobs are scarce. There are few places to buy anything other than necessities. Farming and timbering have reigned supreme from the start, which is one reason the annual median income per capita is only $20,000. Most folks here are hard-working souls who love their families, respect their neighbors, attend church regularly and appreciate their place.

There's nothing special about Lee Avenue's Regional Finance or Security Finance a few doors down, or Lender's Loans, Southern Finance, Credit Central, Local Finance and Tax Service — unless you need them. It's an oasis of quick cash for customers who don't qualify for a long-term loan from the Laffitte family's Palmetto State Bank or the other two banks in town.

A main street fire hydrant is painted bright red and green like a slice of homegrown Hampton County watermelon. The sandy soil is just right for growing watermelons, and local folks have celebrated that fact with an annual harvest festival for 84 years — longer than any other in the state. The curb in front of Regional Finance is freshly painted yellow where what's left of the chicken wing lies amid menthol cigarette butts, a crushed tall-boy malt liquor can, a half-eaten dinner roll and soggy fries. It's the lingering grease and gristle of Rigdon's Fried Chicken, just down the tracks on U.S. Highway 601, that the hovering black fly prefers. Legend has it that engineers braked trains to stop in front of Rigdon's, went inside, grabbed some chicken and a roll before steaming on down the line to Augusta. The restaurant's proprietors still boast that Rigdon's fried chicken is "good enough to stop a train." But there's no stopping now. Drivers of trains are cautious when passing through town thanks to personal injury lawyers associated with the Murdaugh firm.

The fly is also cautious. It spirals up and over Lee Avenue's colorful Palmetto Theater marquee. The refurbished movie house is adjacent to the county's lone venue for the arts. Directly across the street is what's left of Rivers Hardware store, condemned after its roof collapsed. Also gone is the old Loan & Exchange Bank of Hampton, which flew the Confederate battle flag out front until the 1950s when the Laffitte family bought it out. The site has a few park benches where bank patrons arrived early and stood waiting patiently to get in touch with their money.

The house fly drones over to the towering law office on Mulberry Street, between 1st and 2nd East streets. The building was listed as the PMPED law firm back when everyone had a phone book. Prominent lawyers' last-name initials made up the acronym. To locals it was simply "the Murdaugh law firm." They knew exactly where it is, especially if they needed help. In more than a hundred years of practicing law, the firm's lawyers never bothered to hang a shingle. Tall and covered in brick, the law office remains a fortress known colloquially as "CSX Towers" or "The House that CSX Built."

The fly buzzes east past a park and bandstand to the town museum and visitors center, a handsome brick building that once housed the Bank of Hampton on the ground floor and Randolph "Buster" Murdaugh Jr.'s law offices above. It drones across Elm Street (U.S. Highway 278) into the shadows of the courthouse. On this hallowed ground and within these esteemed walls, the Murdaugh family lawyers honed their trade. Large oil portraits of three generations of Randolph Murdaughs hang over the jury box. Each stares down sternly on those whose fates are determined by carefully selected juries of peers.

The fat black fly knows about rotting meat and soggy fries. It knows nothing about Murdaughs, courtrooms, scales of justice, family secrets, hidden treasures, pride, privilege, power and the stench of moral decay and death.

And death is coming soon to the South Carolina Lowcountry.

PART ONE

Randolph Murdaugh III and his family stand on the front steps of the Hampton County Courthouse following a September 2018 presentation of the Order of the Palmetto award. Alex Murdaugh is at the center of the top row. Photo courtesy of *The Hampton County Guardian.*

1

The Grace

See members of the Murdaugh clan, clad in their Sunday best, posed four rows deep on the courthouse steps, smiling for a photo to run in the local newspaper. Solicitor Randolph Murdaugh III clutches his Order of the Palmetto plaque, "in grateful recognition of your contributions and friendship to the State of South Carolina and her people." Earlier that day the homegrown 14th Judicial Circuit solicitor received the state's premier civilian honor for a lifetime of climbing courthouse steps, prosecuting criminals and settling other judicial matters while maintaining his family's lofty socio-political standard and great fortune.

Becoming a member of the Order of the Palmetto is worth the publicity, but it is not exceptionally exclusive. More than four thousand South Carolinians have been asked to join since the Order was established in 1971 by gubernatorial edict, which means many of the picks are political in nature. Randolph Murdaugh III is an example of this. He literally paid his dues after being born to become the lower South Carolina circuit's chief prosecutor, an elected post at the pinnacle of local power and respect. His father and grandfather — both also named Randolph — preceded him in the job, all three serving multiple terms as solicitor with little or no opposition.

"There is probably not a single person whose life has not been influenced by Randolph Murdaugh III. He has contributed the majority of his life to serving the people of Hampton County," gushed circuit resident judge Perry Buckner of Walterboro.

Sheriff T.C. Smalls noted that Murdaugh III had worked to make Hampton County a safe place to live, successfully prosecuting more than 200 murder cases in the district's swath that ranges from coastal Beaufort and Hilton Head Island inland to include towns, communities, farms and swamplands of Beaufort, Jasper, Allendale, Colleton and Hampton counties. For more than eight decades Solicitors Randolph Murdaugh Sr., Randolph "Buster"

Murdaugh Jr. and Randolph "Handsome" Murdaugh III chiefly decided who should be tried, the charges, the punishments and which ones among the guilty deserved mercy. Only seldom did these prosecutors fail to have the support of county grand juries and get the results they wanted.

The Murdaugh men were striking, engaging and talented lawyers. Each performed according to his own script, his own version of the rules of law, in a down-home Southern style. Each knew how to select a jury of so-called peers, and each juror knew he or she had better rule the way the solicitor had encouraged them to do. Each of those Murdaugh solicitors is dead and gone now. Randolph "Randy" Murdaugh IV of Hampton practices law but has shown no interest in running for the office, and likely never will.

Embedded in the Murdaugh solicitors' lineage is a high degree of ambition and self-assuredness at the core of local legend. Hampton County was at the heart of their constituency — their home court — and each was a master of taking advantage of it. Rows upon rows of corn, cotton, soybeans and pine trees far outnumber the men, women and children who plant and cultivate them. The Murdaughs seemed to know each man, woman and child by their first names. Local folks feared and favored them at the same time. Few criticized the family publicly. Power is in the hands of puppeteers, and the Murdaughs were exceptionally good at pulling strings.

A Murdaugh served as the 14th Circuit solicitor for more years than Hampton County has celebrated its beloved Watermelon Festival and parade, which began in 1939. The Murdaugh men's consecutive tenure in elected office is said to have been the longest ever in U.S. history. But the string broke in 2005 when Randolph Murdaugh III retired and his oldest son, lawyer Randolph IV, declined to run for public office. Randolph III's second son, Richard Alexander "Alex" Murdaugh, continued to serve as a badge-carrying, assistant solicitor who equipped his personal vehicle with a panel of police blue lights. He was a volunteer prosecutor when both his wife and youngest son were murdered in June 2019.

During his father's Order of the Palmetto award ceremony, Alex posed for the family photo while standing on the top row alongside his wife and behind his two sons. He smiled slightly as he squinted into the September sun. The photo ran in *The Hampton County Guardian*, and was the last time the Murdaughs were celebrated in public. Today, three people in that photo are dead: Alex Murdaugh's wife, Maggie; his youngest son, Paul; and his father, Randolph III. Almost four years later in March 2023, a jury found Alex guilty of murdering Maggie and Paul. Randolph III died of cancer three days after the killings. The ashes and remains of all three were buried in the Hampton Cemetery on Holly Street while members of the shell-shocked community and media looked on.

But this remarkable family's saga started long ago in another tiny courthouse community more than four hundred miles north of South Carolina's Lowcountry.

2

Reconstruction to Riches

APPOMATTOX COURTHOUSE, VA., April 9, 1865 —

The gray men stand in ragged ranks while history is made, gray in uniform and spirit, young men aged by bullet and blade in the bloody brine of civil war. They shared a thousand campfires but few hot meals and witnessed all manner of death from grapeshot to field guns to gangrene. They are a legion of soldiers who charged boldly into infernal rain of gun fire. They saw mangled men, dead and dying. They carted hundreds of wounded warriors off the killing fields under surgeons' tents onto bloody tables where arms and legs were hacked to halt the rot from spreading.

South Carolinians are among those men standing in ragged gray ranks, no longer cocky young Rebels who fired on Fort Sumter and set their world on fire. Weary and broken they wait for their beloved commander, his hair and beard long and silver, to relinquish his sword, step out from the parlor of grocer Wilmer McLean's house and release them from service to the Confederacy. Mr. McLean knew what the War Between the States was about. His nearby farm was the site of the first Battle of Manassas (Bull Run), which the Confederates easily won. The victory inspired the South, but failed to settle the matter as the Confederate generals had gambled early on. Four years later at Appomattox, defeat etches the ashen faces of the men in gray awaiting the end of a most uncivil war.

Among the vanquished stands Private Josiah Putnam Murdaugh II, 25, of Colleton County in coastal South Carolina, his hand bandaged, still wet and bloodied from battle. Confederate Gen. Robert E. Lee, resplendent in his gray uniform, and members of his staff had arrived at the house earlier that afternoon and waited in the parlor. Crusty chief of U.S. forces Lt. Gen. Ulysses S. Grant, in dirty blue livery and muddy boots, arrived afterward with his assistants to discuss terms of Lee's surrender.

The war was all but over. A tenuous, last-gasp clash by the Confederates brewed not far away in central North Carolina, but the men in Pvt.

Murdaugh's ranks would not participate. They were beaten and worn and ready to return to what was left of their lives.

Later that day Pvt. Murdaugh and the others were thanked by Gen. Lee and dismissed. They could keep their horses and sidearms, if they still had them, along with Gen. Grant's promise of parole, provided they maintained what the federal occupiers deemed acceptable behavior. Young J.P. Murdaugh began his long walk home to the S.C. Lowcountry.

Five days later inside Ford's Theatre in Washington D.C., a blast from an assassin's "pocket-cannon" derringer killed U.S. President Abraham Lincoln, shattering all hope for a kind-and-gentle "reconstruction" of the rebellious South. On April 26, 1865, the Confederacy's cobbled-together Army of Tennessee — the South's last major fighting force — surrendered under Gen. Joseph E. Johnston's command at Durham Station, N.C. When weary J.P. Murdaugh II arrived in the coastal swamplands of South Carolina, he could not imagine the great fortune in store for him and the next four generations of his family.

J.P. Murdaugh II's obituary in 1912 noted he had served the Confederacy in the "famous Hart's Battery, and distinguished himself with utmost ability." It said he was severely wounded in battle but rallied from his injury, still healing, to his post just prior to Lee's surrender. Confederate troop records are difficult to establish at that stage of the war because the ranks were so severely diminished. Men had been quickly moved from one command to fill immediate needs of others. Pvt. Murdaugh served in an artillery battalion of S.C.'s Hampton Legion, organized by Gen. (later Governor) Wade Hampton III in the spring of 1861. Hampton's Legion fought bravely in battles in and around Virginia, and suffered numerous casualties. Hart's Battery was part of the S.C. Horse Artillery Volunteers, later named the Washington Light Artillery, men mostly from the S.C. Lowcountry.

Not long after the war J.P. Murdaugh II moved from Colleton County to Beaufort then to Charleston, where he prospered in phosphate mining and the Lowcountry's commercial fertilizer industry. He further amassed wealth buying and selling real estate in Beaufort and Hampton counties. His properties included a large land acquisition at Almeda, a Hampton County farm community two miles east of Varnville. Almeda became the country home of his line of the Murdaugh clan.

He was a son of Josiah Putnam and Mary Ursala Varn Murdaugh, a member of the family for which Varnville, S.C. is named. J.P. Murdaugh II married Annie Marvin Davis, a cousin of Confederate President Jefferson Davis. When J.P. II's eyes began to fail in 1885, he bought a fine house in Varnville and moved his family to an address listed today as 113 West Carolina Ave. By then Mr. Murdaugh was a well-known money lender. He died in 1912.

The house burned in 1915 and his widow died four years later. Her obituary in the Aug. 6, 1919, issue of *The Hampton County Guardian* noted she was born in Dorchester on a lovely estate as described by popular Charleston novelist William Gilmore Simms. The article asserted she was related to the "great and illustrious statesman" Jefferson Davis and that she had been a loyal daughter of the Confederacy.

The Murdaughs had eight children. Four outlived their parents and two resided in Hampton County until they died. A son, Mortimer, did well in the local grocery and dry goods business. He and his wife, Lynah Newlin Murdaugh, were at the center of society. According to a Varn family history, the Mortimer Murdaugh house was "the focal point for the younger set, for parties and gaiety when their children were in their teens. Seldom have parents done more to enrich the lives of their children with social contacts than did these parents" — which became a long family tradition.

J.P. Murdaugh II's youngest son, Randolph, was born in Varnville on Feb. 28, 1887. He was enrolled briefly at U.S. Naval Academy until health problems were said to have disqualified him from Navy service. He transferred to the University of South Carolina in Columbia where he played on the football team and graduated in 1908. He enrolled in the USC School of Law and graduated in 1910. He was the first of four Randolph Murdaughs to practice law in Hampton, and he wasted no time establishing what became one of the most prominent law firms in South Carolina history.

3

Boat Crash Heard Round the World

BEAUFORT, S.C., Feb. 24, 2019 —

It was just after 2 a.m. and bloody salt water pooled in the well of the crashed powerboat. A teen-age girl was lost in the frigid waters of Port Royal Sound not far from the city of Beaufort. Screams pierced the coastal fog under the Archers Creek bridge to Parris Island. Only moments before, the 17-foot Sea Hunt Triton with six young people aboard hit the span's pilings near the sprawling U.S. Marine Corps' remote east coast recruit depot. Five passengers made it to shore. Mallory Beach, 19, a popular, pretty girl from Hampton, S.C., was lost in the outgoing tide:

"Mallory! Mallory …," her friends' voices echoed through the fog.

The ripped and twisted hull of the single-engine, center-console craft had grounded on the rocks and mud under the bridge. Amid the passengers' enduring shock and panic, a desperate and confused 911 call was made by one of them. Lights and sirens arrived soon afterward. Cellphones rang at parents' homes around the Lowcountry:

"Mom, we can't find Mallory!"
"Dad, there was an accident!"
"Y'all need to come to Beaufort quick!"

Earlier that evening the three young couples had been to a Lowcountry oyster roast at a home on the Chechessee River in Jasper County before departing on a moonlight cruise to waterfront bars in Beaufort. The crash occurred on the way back home. Mallory's body was found floating in marsh a week later near the Broad River Landing, five miles south of the crash site. The horror of it all ripped apart lifelong friends of well-connected families and launched a slew of civil and criminal lawsuits regarding underage drinking, missing money, bank fraud, opioid abuse, two curious "accidental" deaths, and two execution-style murders that made international headlines.

The Archers Creek fiasco began on a chilly Saturday afternoon when the driver of a truck pulling a boat and trailer made a beer stop at Parker's Kitchen convenience store in the Okatie area of Jasper County. The store's surveillance videos show Paul Terry Murdaugh, 19, of Hampton flashing his older brother Buster's ID to purchase Michelob Ultra beer and White Claw hard seltzer. Paul, a case of the contraband in each hand, exited the store and raised his arms in triumph. He packed the drinks in ice-filled coolers in the stern of the boat, got in the truck and drove off. He was joined that day by friends Keith Anthony Cook Jr., 20, and his girlfriend Mallory Madison Beach, 19; Keith's cousin Connor Martin Cook, 19, and date Miley Elaine Altman, 20; and Paul, who was with Morgan Louise Doughty, 20.

Paul's grandfather was Randolph Murdaugh III, a Hampton County lawyer and retired circuit solicitor whose family owned a nearby Chechessee River property nicknamed "Murdaugh Island," which was connected to the mainland by a causeway. Paul and his friends left the island at around 6:30 p.m. in the boat, which belonged to Paul's father, lawyer Alex Murdaugh of Hampton. An hour later they arrived at the dock of Murdaugh family friends James and Kristy Woods, who lived at Carolina Shores on Paukie Island, for the well-attended cookout.

Oysters were steam-roasted, shucked, and slurped straight from the shells or with cocktail sauce and crackers. Also on the menu was a traditional Lowcountry boil — or "Frogmore Stew" — a seasoned mix of shrimp, crabs, sausage, potatoes and corn. Lemonade was served while guests ate, enjoyed a bag-toss game called "cornhole" and played a little basketball. Some made rather discreet trips to and from vehicles and boats for party cups of other beverages. Morgan Doughty sank a basket in a game of "HORSE" so noteworthy that the hostess mentioned it later to investigators.

As the party ended and the temperature fell, Paul and crew declined the Woods' offer to stay the night so they wouldn't "freeze their butts off" going back by water. By midnight Paul and friends were in the boat but he was not ready to go home. He turned his daddy's watercraft north to the waterfront bars of Beaufort, 10 miles away.

A late-night cruise in February along coastal South Carolina is a challenge. As the temperature drops, a thick fog typically rolls in off the warmer waters of the Atlantic Ocean. A salty mist coats the skin and a sulfurous whiff of pluff mud adds "flavor," as the locals say. Paul thrust the throttle forward, the boat's bow rose and the roar of the outboard engine rattled the gunnels. The odor of exhausted oil and spent fuel filled the air until the boat reached a plane. A headwind whipped the riders' hair and buffeted their faces. Running the river in the dark can be deceivingly dangerous, especially when alcohol is in the mix.

The boat crossed the mouth of Broad River before howling inland through Port Royal Sound into the realm of author Pat Conroy's "Prince of Tides." The coolers were half-full of beer and seltzer but the captain craved something stronger. After another mile or two they arrived at the city marina in the heart of historic Beaufort. After securing the boat the group walked next door to the wide waterfront park on Bay Street. Paul talked Connor into accompanying him inside Luther's Rare and Well Done Bar and Grill, which once was the town pharmacy.

Marina security cameras recorded the arrival of the Murdaugh boat and crew. Sweethearts Mallory and Anthony were playful as the group walked through the park and stopped among cozy swings and palmetto branches whispering in the ocean breeze. Music and laughter from inside the nearby bars were also in the air. Snapchat posts they had placed on the Internet and the dockside security videos are the last recorded images of Mallory Beach alive as she stood outside with Anthony and the other girls.

Paul and Connor went straight to Luther's bar and each ordered a "Jager bomb" — a shot of Jägermeister, a German herbal liqueur, in a half-pint of a caffeine-infused energy drink. Each also downed a shot of a vodka-laced "Lemon Drop." They were inside about 10 minutes when Morgan and Miley decided to fetch their dates. In the meantime, Paul accidentally knocked over a bar stool.

"What did that chair ever do to you?" a man sitting at the bar asked Paul.

"What did he say to me?" Paul said to Connor before turning to the stranger and asking the man if he had a problem. Paul was especially cocky when he had been drinking. Connor and the girls hustled Paul outside and the group returned to the boat. Paul staggered along the dock, climbed aboard and sat on the wide captain's bench as the others followed. The engine fired and the lines were loosed. Anthony and Mallory moved to the stern; Morgan and Miley sat at the bow. Connor and Paul shared the console bench while their dates took side seats. Paul grabbed the wheel and off they went.

Miley Altman was Mallory Beach's best friend and the first to tell wildlife officers of the S.C. Department of Natural Resources what had happened: The group left the marina and Paul turned the boat the wrong way, barely missing a moored sailboat, and headed toward the Highway 21 bridge, which connects the city of Beaufort to Lady's Island. Connor snatched the wheel and dodged the pilings.

Alcohol affects people differently. Some seem to do fine. Others become jokers or weepers or lovers or fighters or some sort of combination. Paul Murdaugh got angry when alcohol filled his veins — as if a demon took hold of his brain. His friends called his drunken alter ego "Timmy."

As the boat left Beaufort, Paul removed his jacket and reached toward the night sky. He spread his fingers as wide as he could while the boat roared downriver through the darkness and into the fog. "Timmy is out," his friends quipped at times like this. It was "funny at first," Miley Altman recalled, before the fighting began.

"Let someone else drive," his friends yelled at Paul that night, "Connor knows the way." Paul refused.

"Take us to the closest dock and let us off!" Anthony demanded.

"You think y'all know this river better than me?" Paul responded. "This is my boat … I'll be damned if anyone else drives my damn boat!"

Morgan pleaded with Paul to relinquish the wheel. He sped up the engine then idled it down before releasing the wheel altogether as he argued with his date. Connor took control, steadied the craft. One of the passengers shined a hand-held spotlight forward; another clamped a lamp on the starboard stern cleat.

Paul snatched off his shirt then screamed and cursed Morgan face to face. She pushed him away. "You gonna hit me like all those times before?" she asked. Paul spit on Morgan and slapped her face. She struck him back. Paul snatched the wheel from Connor and slammed the throttle forward. Mallory and Anthony fell into the stern and stayed down for safety. The boat's GPS recorder registered a top speed of almost 30 miles per hour, which is fast on the water, especially on a cold night near the ocean in the Lowcountry.

Anthony told officers he became drowsy as he held Mallory in his arms in the bottom of the boat. But the other passengers vividly recalled what happened next:

"The bridge (over Archers Creek) came out of nowhere," Miley told state investigators. At that point the GPS data recorded the boat's speed at almost 20 miles an hour. "Watch out!" she screamed before impact. Miley, Connor and Morgan were slammed forward but stayed inside the boat. Mallory, Anthony and Paul were ejected into the water, which had chilled to 55 degrees. Hypothermia can set in when seawater is slightly less than 70.

Anthony was skipped like a flat rock thrown side-armed across the water surface toward the bridge. Miley looked up from the bottom of the boat and saw Paul knee deep in water near the shore and Anthony swimming in from farther out. Morgan remembered sitting near the stern and looking downward before falling forward hard onto the deck.

"There's so much blood!" one of the girls screamed from the boat.

"Where's Mallory?" yelled the other.

Connor, his jaw broken and bleeding, managed to call 911 on his cellphone.

Anthony swam back and forth under the bridge searching desperately for his girlfriend. "Mallory, Mallory, oh my God, Mallory," Anthony pleaded into the fog.

Sirens and flashing lights soon flooded darkness above the bridge, while below it the tide swept out swiftly. Only Mallory was missing.

4

A Fearless Prosecutor

Randolph Murdaugh Sr. — *Born: Feb. 28,1887. Died: July 19, 1940*

Greatness radiated from Randolph Murdaugh Sr. — great talent, great ambition, great success and, ultimately, great tragedy. He was the patriarch of the family's lawyers who bore both his first and last names.

His parents, well off by Varnville standards, enrolled Randolph in Hampton County public schools initially and later in a private academy on Orangeburg Highway near the home of headmaster John Timothy Morrison, a former Confederate Army officer, Christian minister and S.C. state legislator.

Randolph received an appointment to the U.S. Naval Academy at Annapolis but left with what was described as a heart problem. He enrolled at the University of South Carolina in Columbia where he earned a bachelor of arts degree in 1908 and his law degree two years later. While at the university, he was an athlete, a member of Sigma Alpha Epsilon social fraternity, and, years later, served on the USC board of trustees.

The ambitious young attorney began his one-man practice a block away from the Hampton County Courthouse. Sepia-toned photos of him standing stiffly in front of the courthouse offer no clue of his dynamic personality. But local lore and newspaper archives combine to offer an in-depth picture of the man.

Legend has it he never hung out a traditional shingle in front of his law office because "everyone knew where the Murdaugh law firm was" — a boast likely started by Murdaugh himself. His practice grew steadily through the years to become Peters Murdaugh Parker Eltzroth and Detrick, PA — or, simply, PMPED — primarily a personal-injury firm with multiple offices that handled cases in 45 of South Carolina's 46 counties. Sound out the firm's acronym and you might get "pimped," an interesting irony.

In 1918 he was a delegate to the S.C. Democratic Convention, and two years later he easily defeated Colleton County lawyers R.M. Jeffries and Heber R. Padgett in the race for circuit solicitor. No one ran against him again, a claim repeated in histories about his law firm.

In 1932 Murdaugh was elected to the state Democratic Party's executive committee, and in 1934 he ran for state chairman before withdrawing to appease fellow party leaders for unspecified reasons. He was a "tried and true Democrat who bows to the will of this convention," declared George Warren, also of Hampton, who had earlier nominated him saying Murdaugh was an able, honest and fearless leader, "an open-minded man not connected with any clique."

Murdaugh had already made local history. Newspaper articles described him as a fearless prosecutor, unafraid to take on people in power including governors, bankers, preachers and sheriffs. He also made headlines while serving on the S.C. Bar Association's grievance committee, which, foxlike, was charged with keeping watch over other lawyers. He soon tried cases against officers of three local banking institutions.

On Sept. 21, 1926, a Hampton County grand jury and Solicitor Murdaugh indicted officers of the Merchants and Planters Bank of Varnville, the Merchants and Planters Bank of Brunson and the Bank of Hampton for violations of state banking laws. The Bank of Hampton building, which later housed Randolph Murdaugh Jr.'s office, currently is the city's museum and visitors center. In February 1928, Randolph Murdaugh Sr. and Hampton lawyer George Warren won convictions of two Beaufort County bankers for making false statements in a conspiracy scandal involving the former Beaufort Bank on Bay Street. The convictions were appealed to the state Supreme Court and upheld.

In July 1930, Murdaugh was appointed by S.C. Attorney General John M. Daniel to represent the state during a special term of court in Lancaster to prosecute two officers of First National Bank and Trust accused of violating state banking laws. Two years prior to that, at the grand opening of the Peoples Bank in Columbia, Murdaugh was listed as a member of its board of directors. The Peoples Bank was affiliated with numerous financial institutions, including the Hampton Banking Company, which had branches in Varnville and Estill in Hampton County, and a branch at Ehrhardt in Bamberg County.

In May 1921, Murdaugh was appointed a local representative of the new First Carolinas Joint Stock Land Bank, which loaned money for improved farmlands and municipal property in both North and South Carolina. *The*

Hampton County Guardian noted that the corporation offered loans "with as little red tape in the matter as possible and with great expedition," adding that Murdaugh was ready at any time to interview those who needed loans. Solicitor Murdaugh obviously profited from his own banking ventures, which would be considered a conflict of interest today.

In April 1921, Murdaugh prosecuted a case against Hampton County Auditor T. Hagood Gooding, accused of incompliance with state tax commission mandates involving unauthorized tax breaks for certain merchants as well as lowered automobile assessments for his friends. In addition to calling numerous expert witnesses to the stand, Murdaugh brought into the courtroom a wagonload of books, papers and records taken from both the auditor's and treasurer's offices that he admitted into evidence. He won the case and the S.C. Supreme Court ordered Gooding to step down and relinquish his files.

The following year and at the request of Gov. Wilson Harvey, Murdaugh prosecuted a case against Colleton County Sheriff W.B. Ackerman on charges of malfeasance regarding "shortages in the finances of his office and missing delinquent tax funds." The sheriff was suspended from office and repaid the missing money but was not convicted. He lost re-election in 1924 and committed suicide before turning over his department's damning financial records to his successor.

Solicitor Murdaugh lost a murder case in 1922 in which Beaufort furniture store dealer Ralph E. Brown was charged with killing Thomas Leonard Perry Bettison, a retired painter and widower with no family in the area. Beaufort County Sheriff James H. Bailey took Brown into custody but did not lock him up in the jail. Instead, Brown stayed overnight inside the sheriff's house. This angered local residents and influential businessmen who petitioned the governor to remove the sheriff from office and demanded the resignations of the mayor, city council members and the police chief.

Sheriff Bailey told *The Beaufort Gazette* the petition was masterminded by his political rivals. He said Brown's wife was hysterical about her husband's arrest so he promised to keep him under his personal guard, adding a comment about the deceased: "Nobody here cared anything about Bettison, an old man who meant little to the business world."

Brown, who was defended by six attorneys, testified that he struck Bettison in self-defense, a claim Murdaugh ridiculed considering the dead man's age.

Brown was acquitted on the murder charge but found guilty of possessing a concealed weapon, and sentenced to 30 days in jail, suspended for good behavior.

Murdaugh tried numerous other unusual cases including a 1928 murder case in Hampton in which a man named Joe Brown was accused of killing James Mauldin, whose "crushed and torn body" was found downtown one morning on the rails between parked boxcars. How the body got there remains a mystery. Solicitor Murdaugh called numerous witnesses, including the train's engineer, who said he saw nobody living or dead on the tracks when he parked the boxcars earlier that day.

Undertaker Eugene M. Peeples testified that very little blood was on or around the tracks, and that he had removed less than a pint from the dead man's body. Witnesses said Brown and Mauldin had fought at a party the night before, and the former beat the latter with a belt. The men were seen later arguing at a service station. The jury rendered a guilty verdict even though it was never determined how Mauldin's body got on the tracks.

Murdaugh was involved in two cases involving S.C. governors. During an Allendale County General Sessions Court session in 1924, he prosecuted former Gov. Wilson G. Harvey, who was president of Enterprise Bank of Charleston, on charges that he accepted deposits while knowing the business was insolvent. The case pitted Murdaugh against Barnwell lawyer Edgar A. Brown, who later was elected a state senator. Sen. Brown became one of a small group of powerful Lowcountry politicians known as "The Barnwell Ring."

Despite objections by the defense, Solicitor Murdaugh placed the former governor in the prisoner's box while the indictment was read, an action considered an insult to the accused. The jury acquitted Harvey, whose attorneys called no witnesses. A year later in an Allendale County case, Solicitor Murdaugh convinced the former governor to plead guilty to lending money to a corporation in which he had financial interests higher than what was allowed by law. In exchange Murdaugh dropped additional charges alleging the former governor loaned money to himself and his brother-in-law. The judge cited Harvey's clean record before sentencing him to either serve four months in prison or pay a $400 fine. The former governor chose the fine.

In August 1931 Solicitor Murdaugh was a defense attorney — which was not his specialty — for Gov. Ira Blackwood before the S.C. Supreme Court.

Gov. Blackwood had called for the removal of Jasper County Sheriff Ben F. Spivey from office after money from his department went missing. But the sheriff refused to step down, saying Gov. Blackwood's demand for his ouster was politically motivated. The high court ruled in the governor's favor. Sheriff Spivey was later convicted in a lower court of stealing the money, served six months in jail and paid a $1,000 fine.

Murdaugh tried a sensational sex scandal in 1927 in Walterboro, the Colleton County seat. The Rev. Lloyd M. Bishop was charged with impregnating an unmarried teen-aged girl in the Cottageville community. The minister, formerly of the Pentecostal Holiness faith, was tried as the Cottageville girl and her infant son attended the trial.

The *Watchman and Southern* newspaper of Sumter reported that the little boy played on the floor near his mother inside the packed courtroom while testimony raged for two days. Probate Judge Ivy A. Smoak had been appointed counsel for the Rev. Bishop. Solicitor Murdaugh and his former political rival Herber R. Padgett represented the state. According to testimony, the preacher did not get along with members of his former congregation so he founded a new church, the chapel of which was built by the Cottageville girl's father.

"There sprang up great intimacy between the two families, and much visiting resulted," the newspaper reported, adding that the pastor won the confidence of the man's 13-year-old daughter, named her one of his personal assistants then licensed her to preach. The paper reported that an illicit relationship developed between the pastor and his young underling which resulted in the child's birth. The girl testified that the Rev. Bishop told her he had fasted and prayed before embarking on their affair and assured her God sanctioned their union.

The defense maintained that the girl, described as the "prosecutrix" in the newspaper, was older than 16, the legal age of consent, when she was impregnated, and suggested another man, who happened to be her relative, was the child's father. Thus it was convenient for her family to fix the blame on the preacher, the defense said. The Rev. Bishop's wife sat by his side throughout the trial, and as the lurid details came to light, it was clear that she was not happy with him.

"The entire courthouse was occupied by white spectators, the Negroes having been excluded from attendance by Judge J. Henry Johnson," the newspaper noted, adding "standing room was at a premium." The Rev. Bishop was found guilty of criminal sexual assault and sentenced up to five years in jail. He served his time and returned to preaching. What happened to the mother and child was never reported.

Randolph Murdaugh Sr. was a life-long Democrat and active in numerous religious and civic organizations. He was a Mason, an Episcopalian and a member of Woodmen of the World, the Benevolent and Protective Order of Elks, the Knights of Pythias and the Junior Order of United American Mechanics. He served on the Hampton County Board of Education from 1915 to 1917 and president/co-owner of the short-lived *Hampton County Herald*. In 1916 he and other local leaders contributed money to purchase clay for a new road from Hampton to Fairfax.

Murdaugh's first wife, Etta Lavinia Harvey Murdaugh, died in 1918. She was the mother of his two children. His second wife, Estelle Marvin Murdaugh, passed away in 1937 when Randolph "Buster" Murdaugh Jr. was a law student at the University of South Carolina. Buster joined his father's practice in 1938 when Randolph Sr. was preparing to run for his sixth term as 14th Circuit Solicitor.

5

DRUNK AS COOTER BROWN

BEAUFORT, Feb. 24, 2019 —

It's Sunday just after 2 a.m. Screams and frantic phone calls pierce the smothering fog over Archers Creek:

"Mom, there are 50 cops here, Coast Guard, everything! They can't find Mallory," an hysterical young person says.

"There's so much blood in the boat," another adds.

"Is this what you wanted? My girlfriend is gone, Bo," Anthony Cook yells at Paul Murdaugh, 19, whose father owns the boat.

Moments earlier, Paul and five of his best friends were in the 17-foot Sea Hunt outboard motor boat as it hummed through dense fog, hit the bridge pilings and careened to a stop atop a bank of rocks. Paul, who never admitted he was driving, along with Anthony, 20, and Mallory Beach, 19, were ejected upon impact. The port side of the hull was gashed and the engine silenced. Blood splattered the deck and puddled in the well. Morgan Doughty, 20, was near the boat's console, blood flowed from her slashed hand. Miley Altman, 20, had minor injuries and remained in the bow. Connor Cook, 19, was also inside the craft, and despite suffering a broken jaw managed to call 911. No one in the boat wore a life jacket.

The bridge "came out of nowhere, next thing I knew we're screaming, and my best friend is missing," Miley Altman later told investigators. Anthony, despite a shoulder injury, swam furiously from one side of Archers Creek to the other searching for Mallory. Paul stood knee deep near the shore and assured his friends that everything would be alright. But everything was not alright — Mallory was missing. As Anthony left the creek, he cursed Paul, shoved him down into the water, then went up on the bridge in a futile effort to spot his girlfriend somewhere out there in the dark.

Paul, stripped down to his boxers, phoned his grandfather — retired 14th

Circuit solicitor Randolph Murdaugh III — and told him what had happened. Capt. Nate Hildreth of the Parris Island Fire and Emergency Service was among the first responders to arrive. He saw Anthony on the bridge and heard him scream at Paul: "I hope you rot in hell ... I hope you die!"

Not long afterward, Cpl. John Keener of the Beaufort County Sheriff's Office escorted Paul to his patrol car and told him to get inside. The cruiser's dash-cam audio picked up the voice of Anthony accusing Paul of driving drunk, saying he deserved to go to prison for life, adding he would get off thanks to his family connections.

The 911 dispatcher was unsure at first precisely where the accident had occurred. A Port Royal police report notes an officer was dispatched at 2:38 a.m. to Archers Creek and Malecon Drive, which connects the mainland to Parris Island. Sheriff's deputies soon gave the dispatcher a description of the missing girl, which was broadcast. Port Royal Police Sgt. Steven F. Reynard assumed command until the arrival of state marine and wildlife officers from the S.C. Department of Natural Resources (DNR), which was in charge of securing the accident scene and conducting the initial investigation because the crash occurred in state waters. They arrived soon afterward, and at 5:30 a.m. Port Royal and Beaufort County police officers were told they could leave the scene.

According to a Port Royal police report, all of the survivors appeared to be intoxicated, although none were tested at the scene. Paul and three of the passengers were taken by ambulance to Beaufort Memorial Hospital. Anthony Cook insisted on staying to search for Mallory. Paul, who had a minor leg injury, was so belligerent in the ambulance that paramedics strapped him down. A state DNR officer later went to the hospital's trauma center to question the survivors.

The fog was so thick that a Coast Guard air search was delayed until sunrise. State divers entered the water at 11 a.m. and volunteers in private boats joined the search. Authorities received numerous calls about possible sightings of the missing girl and likely tidal areas where she might be. But as days passed the shock of family and friends turned to grief. The search was no longer a rescue mission.

"We are moving ... but I don't know that we are moving fast enough for everybody," DNR Capt. Robert McCullough told *The Hampton County Guardian*. He said the divers would soon leave the water but the search would continue until she was found.

Around 1:45 p.m. on March 3, seven days after the crash, Mallory's body was spotted in marsh near the Broad River public boat landing, five miles from the crash scene, by brothers Kenneth and Keith Campbell, who were among the volunteer searchers. Members of Mallory's family, who rarely left the Archers Creek causeway, were summoned to the Beaufort County Coroner's Office, where they identified their daughter's body. The next day an autopsy determined that Mallory had received a blunt-force injury and drowned.

Days later during her funeral in Hampton County, Mallory Beach was described as a bright and kind person with a beautiful smile by her pastor and others. Her obituary noted she was a graduate of Wade Hampton High School, had played on the soccer team and loved animals. She attended Huggin' Oak Church of God in Cummings, enjoyed hunting with her father and worked at the It's Retail Therapy clothing store in Beaufort. The family suggested that memorial gifts be made to the Hampton County Animal Shelter and thanked "all the special operations in Beaufort County for their rescue efforts, and the many friends from Hampton County and surrounding areas for their love, prayers and support."

Specifics about what happened remained as clouded as the fog was that night over Archers Creek. Miley Altman told investigators that Paul Murdaugh was driving when the boat hit the pilings. But Paul steadfastly denied this. Morgan Doughty said Connor Cook might have been at the wheel. His cousin, Anthony Cook, had cursed Paul at the scene and screamed repeatedly, "You killed my girlfriend, Bo." When initially questioned by authorities, Anthony said Paul was driving when they left Beaufort around midnight. Later he said he was not sure who was at the wheel when the boat hit the pilings.

That morning at the hospital, state DNR Cpl. Austin Pritcher asked Paul if he was driving when the accident occurred. "Why do you need to know who was driving?" Paul responded, adding it would not help to find Mallory. When asked again, Paul said, "I definitely was not driving."

Paul was loud, cursing, rude and uncooperative in the ambulance and in the hospital. A female emergency room technician requested a urine sample from him. He asked her to "hold it for him" then pointed to her buttocks and said, "Wow, that's nice." The on-duty physician said Paul was so intoxicated he could hardly stand up. Paul tried to rip off a heart monitor and demanded his clothes so he could leave the hospital. Cpl. Pritcher asked Paul to take a blood/alcohol test. Paul declined. A later check of Paul's ER medical record noted a routine blood test administered at 4 a.m., two hours after the crash, showed his serum had an ethanol level of 286.1 mg/dL, which is more than three times the legal alcohol limit.

Among those who arrived early at the hospital that morning were Paul's father, Alex, and his grandfather, Randolph Murdaugh III — both lawyers well versed in legal defense and damage control. They interrupted Cpl. Pritcher's interview with Paul, and advised their son/grandson he did not have to give a statement at that time.

"I'm talking to Paul," Cpl. Pritcher protested.

Retired solicitor Randolph Murdaugh III fired back, "I'm his lawyer, starting now … He isn't giving any statement."

Alex Murdaugh, who had hung a solicitor badge from his pants pocket before entering the ER facility, introduced himself to the staff and checked the tracker board that listed names and room numbers of the passengers. Staffers said Alex reeked of alcohol as he went from room to room saying he needed to advise each passenger on what to say and not say to investigators. Alex stopped Connor Cook in the hall as the young man with a broken jaw was taken by wheelchair to get a CT scan. "We're going to figure everything out," Alex tried to assure Conner. A hospital security guard later overheard Alex telling someone on his cellphone: "She's gone; don't worry about her."

Cpl. Pritcher left Paul and went into Morgan's room. Later, when Alex tried to enter, Morgan told Pritcher the only other person she wanted in the room was her mother. She asked the officer to close the curtain, saying, "I don't want anybody else to hear what I'm going to say." Morgan had earlier told police she thought Connor was driving because Paul was too drunk to do so. In the hospital, she asked Cpl. Pritcher if she could clarify her initial statement "now that my head is on right." He agreed. She told him she did not know for sure who was driving when the accident occurred.

In days that followed, newspapers cranked out stories about the accident while the wheels of justice turned slowly in the 14th Judicial Circuit. Two judges close to the Murdaugh family declined to participate in the case, and 14th Circuit Solicitor Isaac "Duffie" Stone recused himself in a letter submitted a day after the crash to S.C. Attorney General Alan Wilson. Stone wrote that two of the passengers were relatives of people employed by his office, and he also noted that Alex and his father had served as part-time assistant solicitors for him in the Hampton County office.

On March 25 the Beaufort County sheriff recused himself and his entire department from further involvement in the investigation because of long-standing, close ties to the solicitor's office. Only the S.C. Department of Natural Resources remained to investigate the case. DNR agents gathered GPS data on the boat; interviewed some of the passengers as well as officers, paramedics and firefighters who responded to the crash; obtained alcohol sales receipts from Parker's Kitchen convenience store and Luther's Rare and Well Done Bar and Grill; and gathered surveillance footage from the store, the bar and the dock of Beaufort's downtown marina.

Miley and Morgan gave statements to DNR officers soon after the crash and in follow-up interviews. Anthony declined to participate at that time. DNR agents did not interview Connor or Paul, a department spokesperson said, because each had attorneys who had advised them to not say anything.

The Hampton County Guardian reported in April that it had been 38 days since the crash, charges had yet to be filed and no one had admitted to driving the boat when it hit the bridge. Readers of the hometown newspaper and others could not help but wonder if justice would ever be served. It was no secret the Murdaugh lawyers were involved.

6

Train Trouble

I was drunk the day my moma got out of prison
And I went to pick her up in the rain
But before I got to the station in my pickup truck
She got ran over by a damned old train.

— Singer and songwriter David Allan Coe

Randolph Murdaugh Sr.'s father, the Confederate soldier Josiah Putnam Murdaugh II, prospered in the post-Civil War phosphate mining and commercial fertilizer industry around Charleston before going into the real estate business in Beaufort and Hampton counties. During the Great Depression he lived on a farm with his family two miles east of Varnville in an area called Almeda. Among their neighbors was E.R. "Little Ed" Ginn, whose father, a state senator, owned a farm and a sawmill. The Depression hit rural South Carolinians hard but the Ginns and the Murdaughs were better off than most thanks in part to the railroad tracks that cut through their properties. The railroad was the life blood of the community; it provided a way to ship farm products and timber to bigger markets.

According to Rose-Marie Eltzroth Williams' history of Varnville titled *Railroads and Sawmills*, Little Ed Ginn rode the rails as a boy to Frog Hollow and Varnville and back delivering cornmeal, cane syrup and stove wood to families along the way. Little Ed was 18 years old the day the train did not stop as usual at Almeda, so he decided to jump off and walk back to his house. He leaped from the train but got himself hung up between two freight cars and was thrown to the ground beside the tracks. Young Randolph Murdaugh saw the accident, ran to the scene and carried his injured friend to the Ginns' house. The next day S.C. Sen. E.R. Ginn arrived home from the Statehouse in Columbia, then drove his son to a Charleston hospital where Little Ed survived, after losing a leg to a surgeon's saw.

Randolph was fresh out of the University of South Carolina School of Law in 1910 when he founded his one-man law practice in downtown Hampton. Four years later he married Etta Lavinia Harvey, a daughter of local physician Dr. Joseph Brantley Harvey, and they had two sons, Randolph Jr. and John Glenn, before she died in 1918. But Randolph Sr.'s ascent to success never slowed. Murdaugh, like later generations of lawyers bearing his name, was popular among citizens — those deemed to be on the right side of the law.

The making of the Murdaugh legend began in the courtrooms of that era with this rising star among Southern prosecutors. "Grand Jury Lauds Murdaugh," a February 1940 headline in the local newspaper said, and the story included an editorial endorsement of Randolph Sr.'s re-election as district solicitor. His name and that of his second wife peppered the hometown paper from front to back.

Randolph Sr. was involved in a variety of local and state affairs. He prosecuted criminals and seldom lost a case. He helped pay for the clay to build a road from Hampton west to Fairfax. He briefly published his own newspaper. His family's comings and goings appeared often on the society pages.

Randolph Sr. got together regularly with his buddies, and he especially enjoyed playing poker with them. But tragedy bore down at high speed at 1 a.m. on July 9, 1940 when Solicitor Murdaugh drove home from a card game in Yemassee. He stopped his car at the Camp Branch railroad crossing east of Varnville as a westbound train steamed through the darkness toward Augusta. The engineer, W.W. Bartlett, did not notice Murdaugh's car until the train was forty yards away. As the engine's headlight fully illuminated the crossing, Bartlett saw Murdaugh in his car. Randolph appeared to be waving at the train from the driver's side window. Suddenly his car lurched forward and stopped dead on the tracks. "The impact hurled the automobile approximately 900 feet up the track, totally wrecking it," according to *The Hampton County Guardian.* "Murdaugh's body was found beside the tracks approximately 150 feet from the crossing." Solicitor Randolph Murdaugh Sr. was only 54 years old when he perished.

Friends and family knew that Randolph had suffered some sort of health issue for about a year, and had been released from the hospital two months before he died. Was his health a factor? A suicide perhaps? Was he driving home drunk from the poker game? Did his car malfunction? A coroner's jury ruled the death simply as an accident. But Murdaugh family members were suspicious.

7

THE GENTLEMAN'S TREATMENT

BEAUFORT, S.C., April 18, 2019 —

Beaufort County's grand jury indicted Paul Murdaugh on three felony charges related to the Archers Creek crash, including one that he drove the boat under the influence of alcohol that night and ultimately was responsible for Mallory Beach's death. But Paul was not arrested. He was simply summoned to court for his arraignment and bond hearing on Monday, May 6, and the charges against him were filed simultaneously.

Reporters asked the obvious question: Was special treatment given the young member of Hampton's prominent family of lawyers? S.C. Attorney General's Office spokesman Robert Kittle responded: "He is not being given special treatment," adding Paul had an attorney and was charged directly by the grand jury. This did not sit well with the public. "Why wasn't the man accused in Mallory Beach's death arrested?" asked WSAV, a Savannah television station. Other reporters asked the same thing.

Paul's indictment and bond hearing occurred as scheduled inside the Beaufort County Judicial Center. Fifteenth Circuit Judge Steven John presided and Columbia lawyers Jim Griffin and state Sen. Dick Harpootlian represented young Murdaugh. The courtroom was packed. Paul wore a plaid shirt, blue sport coat, khaki pants and topsiders. He said nothing during the hearing, which lasted less than 15 minutes. A court officer holding handcuffs approached Paul but a prosecutor waved her off. Paul's booking photograph was soon snapped in a courthouse hallway. He entered a plea of not guilty on all three counts and was released on a $50,000 personal recognizance bond. He surrendered his passport but the judge denied a prosecutor's request to require him to wear GPS-locating and alcohol-monitoring devices. He never set foot in jail.

Paul was told he could travel only within the five-county 14th Circuit, but during a bond reconsideration hearing, Judge Michael Nettles, of Florence, allowed him to attend classes at the University of South Carolina in Columbia and to confer with his attorneys there. He was prohibited from having any contact with the other boat crash victims or their family members, which was standard procedure. Paul later was spotted by folks not only in Columbia and Hampton but also in the Upstate and out with friends in Charleston.

The editor of *The Hampton County Guardian* sat two rows behind Paul's parents, Alex and Maggie Murdaugh, during the arraignment hearing. "How ya doing?" Alex turned and asked the hometown editor, while Maggie sat silently beside her husband. Members of Mallory Beach's family were there but did not address the court. Following the arraignment, Mallory's father, Phillip Beach, told *The Hampton County Guardian*: "We are trusting in the Lord in this whole ordeal and asking every Christian in this nation to pray that God's will, and justice, be done. Regardless of the outcome, nothing will bring her back, but we do have the assurance of seeing her again one day. All we want now are prayers for her, and for the defendant and his family as well."

The public reaction was mixed. "Prayers answered: Man charged in Beaufort Co. boat crash that killed Mallory Beach," a headline in *The State* newspaper said. In a blistering editorial, the *Island Packet*'s Liz Farrell wrote: "No cuffs. No jumpsuit. No jail. Paul Murdaugh gets a gentleman's treatment in a S.C. court." The maximum penalty for felony boating under the influence of alcohol is $25,000 and 25 years in prison. But Paul Murdaugh never saw the inside of a courtroom again, and no one has been found criminally liable for Mallory's death.

8

RANDOLPH JR. TAKES CHARGE

HAMPTON COUNTY, Oct. 1, 1940 —

Randolph Murdaugh Sr. was dead, killed by a Charleston & Western Carolina freight train. His son, Randolph "Buster" Murdaugh Jr., took over the Murdaugh & Murdaugh firm and, as executor of his father's will and estate, filed a wrongful-death lawsuit against the train company in the Hampton County Court of Common Pleas on behalf of widow Mary Murdaugh and her children.

It alleged that the train was traveling from Yemassee to Varnville at a high rate of speed and failed to blow a whistle or ring a bell at the Camp Branch crossing. The suit also alleged the crossing and its approaches were in washed out and dangerous condition, and that Randolph Sr.'s view was obscured by trees and tall underbrush on that foggy night, placing him in sudden and imminent peril.

Buster Murdaugh demanded a judgement of $100,000 for the death of his father, about $2 million today. A settlement was reached a year later. The payoff secured the Murdaugh family legacy of influence that impacted thousands of people and businesses for the next 82 years. Thanks primarily to the Murdaughs, Hampton County became known by defense attorneys as a "judicial hellhole" in the swamps of South Carolina's Lowcountry.

The Murdaugh firm handled both criminal and civil cases through the years and amassed the family's as well as future partners' fortunes by mostly settling injury cases. Clyde Eltzroth joined the firm in 1952, "read the law" under Randolph Jr. and eventually became a circuit judge without having a law-school degree. In March 1956, the firm also added J. Robert Peters Jr. as a partner.

The Murdaugh, Eltzroth and Peters law firm grew through the years. At the height of its power, the firm became Peters Murdaugh Parker Eltzroth and Detrick, or simply PMPED, with offices across the state. It directly employed a dozen lawyers and more than 50 support workers. PMPED's reputation for defending "the little guy" against corporate giants became nationwide. The firm represented a variety of clients: farmers against seed companies, slip-and-fall victims against big-box retailers, critically injured motorists or their survivors against vehicle and tire manufacturers, and, ironically, people hit by trains.

Most of Randolph Sr.'s male children, grandchildren and great-grandchildren either managed or worked in the family law practice. However, by the year 2013 the patriarch's great-grandson, lawyer Richard Alexander Murdaugh, who was 45 at that time, was quietly stealing money from the firm's partners and clients in a multi-million-dollar crime spree that eventually proved disastrous.

9

Justice Now Center Stage

HAMPTON, S.C., May 2019 —

Mallory Beach was a student at the University of South Carolina in Columbia when she died Feb. 24 in the Beaufort boat accident. She was attractive, energetic and well loved by family and friends. It took a week for searchers to find her body, and the lingering question about who was driving when Alex Murdaugh's family motorboat hit the bridge ignited suspicion about how authorities were handling the high-profile case. The Murdaugh name evoked power, privilege, money and land in the S.C. Lowcountry, and local folks wondered how the prominent family of lawyers would finagle the facts to protect Alex and Maggie's youngest son, Paul, who had been drinking and more than likely driving when the accident occurred.

The Murdaugh family had developed long-standing ties with wildlife agents and others in the state Department of Natural Resources through the years. Alex had invited several of them to hunt wild hogs, deer and birds at Moselle, his 1,700-acre estate on the Big Salkehatchie River. In return, Alex called on them for help in a variety of matters mostly concerning protection of his land holdings, preservation of wildlife, hunting and fishing. Now DNR officers were investigating allegations of young Paul's wild and wooly role in the deadly accident.

Mallory had been missing for more than a week in the vicinity of historic Beaufort, the famed Parris Island Marine Corps Recruit Depot, and Hilton Head Island's popular resorts and world-class golf courses. A wide range of people nationwide had heard or read about Mallory's death. Why were details scarce? Was it a coverup?

The investigation — or the lack thereof — galled the Beach family, Mallory's friends and a growing number of others. Empathy ran deep for Mallory's parents, who had waited and prayed day and night on the causeway near the bridge as hope of finding their child alive evaporated. A March 8, 2019, headline in Hilton Head's *Island Packet* declared: "Justice now center stage in boat wreck that killed teen, rocked Beaufort and S.C. Lowcountry." *Packet* columnist David Lauderdale asked readers if justice was possible considering the Murdaugh family's prominence in the 14th Judicial Circuit, and called on the FBI to investigate the case.

Reporters Mandy Matney and Liz Farrell of the *Island Packet* and the *Beaufort Gazette* wrote about events leading up to Mallory's death as well as close relations between the Murdaughs and state wildlife and marine officers who were at the crash scene. One agent had recently played in a golf tournament with Murdaugh family members; another was a close friend of Paul's uncle John Marvin Murdaugh. The wife of a third officer was a former Murdaugh employee who had reportedly been to the family's river house on several occasions. Questions persisted about why officers failed to administer sobriety tests on the passengers, especially Paul, at the crash site.

DNR spokesman David Lucas said that, by the time department officers arrived, all the passengers except for Anthony Cook and his missing girlfriend had been taken to the hospital. Lucas later noted that field sobriety tests are typically delayed if the driver had injuries needing prompt medical attention. Everyone agreed that both Paul Murdaugh, who had injured his leg, and Connor Cook, whose jaw was broken, had driven the boat at different times that night, but it was not clear who was at the wheel when it hit the pilings.

Three months later state DNR investigators had yet to question Paul, who had taken his friends out that night on his father's boat. While some of the best journalists in Beaufort and Charleston counties rooted out a few more details about the crash, it wasn't until after investigative reporter John Monk of *The State* newspaper in Columbia arrived in Hampton that the initial wave of questions intensified to become a howling tsunami.

Monk had reported in the Carolinas for almost 50 years — so long ago that children of his first good sources were among his best contacts now. Polite and professional yet persistent and aggressive, he walked Hampton's main street, talked to local folks and eventually collected a trove of information about the Murdaughs.

After college and a stint in the Army, Monk worked as a newspaper reporter in South Carolina's Georgetown and Horry counties before joining *The Charlotte (N.C.) Observer* in 1979. He was among the first journalists on the ground to cover the U.S. invasion of Panama in 1989 that deposed and ultimately jailed de-facto leader and drug smuggler Manuel Noriega. Not long afterward, Monk interviewed anti-Sandinista guerrillas in the Nicaraguan mountains and wrote of their attempts to remove leftist strongman Daniel Ortega from power. Monk worked in the *Observer's* Washington, D.C. bureau covering politics, civil rights and other issues before joining *The State* in 1996. He built on his reputation as a good investigative reporter covering numerous murder trials, passage of a mandatory state seatbelt law, politics, race relations and the environment.

"Hampton seemed like a sleepier-than-usual old town with its best days behind it … once a bustling place on the railroad line from somewhere important to somewhere important," Monk recalled. "One thing that stood out was the Murdaugh law firm's building, a structure in red brick, black shutters and white-trimmed windows that reminded me, despite its dignified appearance, of a fortress. I knew instantly it held a lot of secrets. I regretted I didn't have time in the spring of 2019 to pry into those secrets. I loved its nickname — 'The House that CSX built' — so I hunted down the editor of the Hampton paper to chat him up."

On April 5, 2019, *The State* published an article titled "Powerful S.C. family faces scrutiny following boat crash that killed 19-year-old woman," written by John Monk and Cody Dulaney. It was an exposé on the Murdaughs and their powerhouse law firm. It unearthed past scandals about the flamboyant late solicitor Randolph "Buster" Murdaugh Jr., and touched on more recent crimes and unsolved deaths connected to the family. The world beyond sleepy Hampton, S.C. was exposed to what the locals already knew: the Murdaughs had a long history of using their wealth, reputation, influence and knowledge of the law to wield enormous power.

The story quickly got more than 90,000 clicks on digital media. "People sensed that the family's dynamics — money, power, politics etc. — offered glimpses into dark, unexplored regions of the human soul. Readers wanted more, they got more, and it's still not over," Monk said. Was the great-great-grandson of family patriarch Randolph Murdaugh Sr. being protected by local authorities? Years of smooth sailing ended for the Murdaughs as the winds of change whipped into a steady howl in the family's ears.

10

THE ROOSTER CROWS

"I'm the cock of the walk in this part of South Carolina..."
— Randolph "Buster" Murdaugh Jr.

HAMPTON, S.C. —

A broken-down woman sobs on the broken-down couch in the front room of a broken-down shack. A smeared drip of nosebleed does not hide the slap mark that would be another tell-tale bruise on her face tomorrow.

"If you come in this house, I'm a kill the bitch!" a man screams through the ripped screen of the front door as local lawmen hunch behind squad cars in the yard. The man pokes the twin barrels of a shotgun through the screen to show he means business, steps back and shoves it to the back of his wife's head, mashing her face into the couch's stained fabric. "I ought'a shoot ya anyway, you lying-ass whore!"

A broken swing and collapsed plastic pool are out in the yard too, but the children are gone ... fled to safety of the neighbor's house like many times before. A dog growls from beneath an old car on blocks; hunting hounds howl from a filthy pen out back. Megaphone in hand, the sheriff tries to cajole the man into releasing his wife.

"Get the hell out of my yard before I shoot you all!" the man responds. The lawmen, handguns and rifles in their hands, hunker down further behind their cruisers in case the drunkard has buckshot in his shotgun. One laughs nervously as he peeps over the hood. All are wary, wondering if the man will make good on his threats.

A familiar Cadillac rolls up and stops behind them. Out steps a stocky, stern-faced man in a business suit. He has a wad of tobacco in his cheek. Solicitor Randolph "Buster" Murdaugh Jr. wasn't one to sit around waiting to add another killing to his docket. He spits a mouthful of tobacco juice on the ground and turns to one of the deputies, a red-headed country boy:

"Son, run over to my house and see my wife."

"What you want me to say?"

"Tell Gladys I'll be late for supper." The solicitor flashed a wide, tobacco-stained grin. "She don't need to know nothin' else."

Randolph Murdaugh Jr.'s mother died in 1918, when he was three years old. Soon afterward his father married the second of three wives. It wasn't long until the boy tagged along with his father from courthouse to courthouse, trial to trial, watching and learning how to be a solicitor like his dad. "He had been both father and mother to me," Randolph Jr. said years later after Randolph Sr. died.

The son grew up hunting and fishing alongside his father. He excelled in football, baseball and boxing while attending Varnville public schools. He won all of his boxing matches at the Varnville Pavilion until 1931, when he lost a highly publicized bout against K.O. Kuler of Allendale by a technical knockout in the fourth round. Young Randolph soon learned that losing a boxing match was nothing compared to losing a fortune in the stock market. Randolph Sr. was a gambling man who lost almost everything when the banks failed the following year. Fortunately, his son, an outstanding running back at Varnville High School, received a full scholarship to play football at the University of South Carolina. He weighed 180 pounds when he became a Gamecock and beefed up to 240 pounds by his senior year when he played the guard position. His coaches dubbed the short, stocky, exceptionally strong lineman "Buster" because of his ability to deliver savage blocks to his opponents.

Buster was popular at USC. He participated in campus politics, joined campus organizations and played on both the football and baseball teams. He was elected to the university's athletic advisory board when he was a freshman, and became treasurer of the German Club. He was appointed a S.C. Senate clerk in 1937, graduated from the USC School of Law in 1938 and joined his father as a partner in the Murdaugh & Murdaugh law firm.

His father died two years later when hit by the train. Randolph Jr. took charge of the firm, sued the railroad company, got a healthy, undisclosed settlement and restored the family wealth. He had been appointed by Gov. Burnett Maybank to fill his father's job as district solicitor until the next election, which he won easily, and served 11 consecutive terms — which he claimed to be longer than any other officeholder in U.S. history. He faced opposition only in 1940, 1952 and 1962. His opponent in 1940 and 1952 was W.J. "Stump" McLeod, a WWII veteran of Walterboro. Buster ran unopposed in 1944 and 1948 then won handily every four years until retiring in 1986.

A political advertisement in the June 18, 1952, issue of *The Hampton County Guardian* praised Buster Murdaugh as an experienced, aggressive and fearless candidate devoted to duty above personal interests. It said he had prosecuted 2,693 criminal cases, and 2,596 of them were either convictions or the accused had pleaded guilty. Buster also bragged that his conviction average was as high or higher than any prosecutor in the nation. In announcing his candidacy for solicitor in 1956, Buster touted a 95 percent conviction rate while heaping praise on local lawmen for their help. Publicity-starved police officers loved him for it.

For years Buster welcomed folks to the Hampton County Watermelon Festival alongside numerous state and national legislators from South Carolina. He was especially proud to have been the grand marshal of the 1987 festival parade. Buster knew exactly how to play small-town politics to his own advantage.

A lifelong Democrat like his father, Murdaugh served as Varnville mayor pro tem, vice chairman of the Hampton County Welfare Board, president of the county's Young Democratic Club and executive committeeman of the county party for 45 years. He was president of the 14th Judicial Circuit Bar Association, president of the State Junior Bar Association, president and president emeritus of the S.C. Solicitors' Association, a founding member of the S.C. Trial Lawyers Association, vice president of the S.C. Bar Association, and the first S.C. director of the National Prosecuting Attorneys Association. He was a 32nd degree Mason, a Shriner, War Fund chairman of the American National Red Cross, director of the Furman Farm Loan Association, a member of both the Lions and Ruritan civic clubs, an officer in the S.C. National Guard and chairman of the board of stewards of the Varnville United Methodist Church.

Author Pat Conroy grew up in Beaufort and wrote highly personal novels and memoirs set in the S.C. Lowcountry that inspired popular motion picture films. His novels included *Conrack, The Lords of Discipline, The Great Santini* and *The Prince of Tides*. Conroy first met Buster Murdaugh inside the Hampton County Courthouse. The author-to-be had been fired by the Beaufort County School Board as a teacher of young African-American students on remote Daufuskie Island, and he was in court trying to get his job back. Conroy failed to do so, but during the proceedings the future best-selling author spotted an older man seated near the jury box who "laughed his ass off" at some of his comments.

The man introduced himself as Solicitor Randolph "Buster" Murdaugh Jr.:

"I'm the cock of the walk in this part of South Carolina, and, boy, you know how to put on a show," Buster said. After lighting a cigar, he asked Conroy to join the Murdaugh law firm. "I'll send you to law school and make you the god-damnedest lawyer you've ever seen." But Conroy politely declined.

By then Buster was a Lowcountry legend. While his work ethic earned him "mountains of respect, tons of admirers," as one newspaper reported, his likeable character as an exuberant Southern lawyer had set him apart. The courtroom was his stage and he might do or say anything from the center of it. He often threatened to quit on the spot if juries failed to convict and execute people he prosecuted for murder. The jurors believed him.

Puffed up by success and public adoration, Buster strutted Lowcountry halls of justice and attracted large crowds, especially when accused killers' lives were on the line. He dressed sharp and talked out the side of his mouth because he always had a wad of Red Man tobacco protruding from his cheek or an unlit cigar between his teeth. His oratory was Southern and exceptional, often witty and endearing, sometimes heated and blunt. It's been said so often it might be true that after a judge told him to stop spitting in the courtroom if he couldn't hit the spittoon, Buster packed up his files and left, effectively shutting down the proceedings. He agreed to return after the judge relented — or so the story goes.

Murdaugh was also a good plaintiff's attorney. Fourteenth Circuit Judge Clyde Eltzroth and a former Murdaugh law partner, described Buster as "the finest trial lawyer I ever saw ... I never knew him to refuse help to anyone who asked." Assistant Solicitor Steve Knight agreed: "You could learn more about prosecuting cases in five minutes from Mr. Buster than you could in years at law school."

Murdaugh also earned the respect of his district's farmers and other working-class citizens. He was as comfortable talking to them as he was to South Carolina judges, senators, governors and others in power. He studied people carefully and convinced them his primary goal was to serve all who needed him. Indeed, it was difficult to seat a jury in his district that would not rule his way. That's because local folks loved and feared him at the same time. It's why Buster Murdaugh never lost a race for solicitor in 46 years.

"He could talk to the mother of a man who had just gotten the death penalty, and she would thank him for it," Hampton County historian Sam Crews III said. Typically around supper time, Buster would stop in to visit friends, especially when he knew Gladys was serving leftovers. His hosts invariably asked the affable solicitor to stay and eat. Afterward, Buster would declare it was the best meal he had ever had. If offered a whiskey, he seldom declined, always claiming the brand happened to be his favorite. That meant something to his hosts, Crews said.

Legend has it that Buster sometimes meted out justice on his own. He kept a stack of drivers' licenses wrapped in rubber bands inside his desk drawer. If you were a friend, or simply someone he deemed worthy of a second chance, and charged with, say, drinking and driving, Buster would add your license to the stack. If you behaved for what he considered an appropriate length of time, he would drop the charges and return your license. He sealed lots of friendships that way.

He enjoyed socializing with judges, sheriffs and other law enforcement officers, bought them drinks, invited them to hunt, fish and special barbecues on this property. One of his fishing buddies was Jasper County Sheriff Randy Blackmon. A retired Lowcountry game warden who asked to remain anonymous recalled catching a 14th Circuit judge violating state hunting laws during an organized dove shoot. The judge was ankle deep in cracked corn (baiting the birds was illegal in South Carolina at that time), and wrote the man a ticket. But Buster, his pockets stuffed with dead birds, saw what was happening and walked across the field toward them. The warden tore up the citation and said, "I might write a circuit judge a ticket, but I'll be damned if I'm going to give Buster Murdaugh one."

Buster steadily grew his friendships and his family's personal-injury practice while prosecuting cases ranging from moonshine production and sales to rapes and capital murders. Upon retirement he claimed he worked an average of 2,000-plus cases annually and won most them.

One of his first big murder cases was in 1948 when he prosecuted an Estill shopkeeper who used a baseball bat to beat to death his wife and two of their young children. Prior to the killings, the man had been twice committed to the state mental hospital Columbia, treated and released. A neighbor testified that on the night of the murders, he heard the children crying, a dog barking and what sounded like a someone wielding a sledgehammer inside the house next door. The killings were so brutal that they made headlines as far away as Sioux Fall, S.D., where *The Daily Argus-Leader* reported that the killer waited for his family to return from a movie theater before beating one after the other. Two days later, the accused was again taken to the mental hospital. The acting superintendent of the institution said the man suffered from "alcoholic psychosis with acute hallucinosis," and was a threat to humanity when drunk.

Buster told *The Hampton County Guardian* he had asked that the man be kept in the asylum, adding, if returned to stand trial, "it would be just another murder case to me." The accused was returned. The first trial — for killing the son — began at 9:30 a.m. inside the Hampton courthouse. The boy and his mother were dead when Estill physician Dr. Johnson Peeples arrived at the scene. He said the girl had a crushed skull but was still breathing when taken to the Ridgeland hospital, where she died.

At one point in the proceedings, Buster offered a dramatic demonstration of how the bat was wielded during the murders. Historian Sam Crews, who was nine years old at that time, worked as a jury boy for five dollars a day. He said Murdaugh swung the bat hard and violently as he presented it as evidence. When he was through talking to the jury, he handed the bat to young Crews. The judge was not impressed. He called Buster to the bench for a conference, after which he summoned Crews' mother to take the boy from the courtroom, and the trial resumed.

Defense attorney, C.B. Searson, argued that his client was insane and needed medical care, not the electric chair. "He destroyed his family when he was in a condition for which he was not responsible. Give him a chance." In response, Buster called witnesses who testified they were inside a nearby store when in walked the killer, with the bloody bat in hand, and announced, "I just killed my old lady." Buster warned the jury: "If he is ever released on society and kills again, no one is responsible but yourselves."

They began deliberating at 4:40 p.m., returning once to hear the court stenographer read medical testimony about the man's condition. At 1 a.m. the twelve-man jury — women could not serve then — found the man guilty of killing his son, and recommended mercy when sentenced. The judge gave him life in prison. He was also convicted of killing his wife and daughter, and got two more life sentences, all three to run consecutively.

Murdaugh prosecuted another highly publicized murder case in which a Fairfax man waited until after jury selection had begun before pleading guilty of cutting the telephone line to an elderly widow's residence, going inside, stabbing her to death and sexually assaulting the corpse. Buster reluctantly agreed to accept the plea after the woman's family requested leniency. The man got life plus 80 years.

In 1970 Murdaugh brought to trial five well known white men accused of killing a young black man during a time of intense racial unrest in the area. Newspapers dubbed the accused the "Fairfax Five." The jury of seven blacks and five whites deliberated for only an hour before finding two of the five not guilty, and dropping charges against the other three. Observers wondered if a fix was in on the jury.

In 1979 Buster prosecuted two white men from Pennsylvania for the rape, torture and murder of a 33-year-old black woman on St. Helena Island in Beaufort County. The men, along with two young white girls (one only 11 years old), were in a car headed for the beach when they picked up Betty Gardner, who was hitchhiking from her house to work in a nearby tomato field. She was driven to a wooded area and forced to have oral sex with both men and the older girl, raped by the men, stabbed with a knife, slashed across her neck with a broken bottle, had KKK carved on her chest, then strangled to death with a piece of garden hose. The underage girl was too young to be tried for murder, and the older girl was given immunity to testify as an eyewitness against the men — John Arnold and John Plath.

At one point during the trial Buster asked the older girl to tie a piece of garden hose around his neck, then cross-examined witnesses for the defense while describing in brutal detail how the victim was tortured and killed. At one point Buster got on his back on the floor in front of the jury box and re-enacted the woman's death while splaying out his arms and legs. Both men were found guilty.

During the sentencing phase, Buster pointed to Plath and told the jury: "It's a joke to him … that man doesn't think y'all have got the guts to kill him." He also vowed he would never again seek the death penalty against anyone in the county if the jury did not vote to execute both killers. The jurors, some teary-eyed, voted to do just that.

Beaufort lawyer Scott Graber, who defended John Arnold, later wrote in the *Island Packet* that he had asked the state Supreme Court to set aside the first trial primarily because Buster had threatened to never seek the death penalty again in the county if the jury did not vote to execute the men. A second trial in Beaufort was conducted four years later by a different judge, jury and prosecution team. Both men were found guilty again, and Plath and Arnold were executed by lethal injection in 1998.

In a 1986 trial that Murdaugh prosecuted and won in Jasper County, the jury deliberated only 90 minutes before rejecting the death penalty for two men and a woman convicted of a murder linked to a local drug war. Henry Mitchell, 24, Eric Robinson, 19, and Wanda Battiste, 22, were each sentenced to life imprisonment in the shooting death of Scottie Miles of Ridgeland. Mitchell admitted he used two handguns to shoot Miles five times in the head. The trio were also charged with killing Myron Cleland, 24, of Ridgeland. Mitchell testified that he accidentally dispatched Cleland with a blast from a sawed-off shotgun.

Murdaugh was not happy that the killers were spared the death penalty. "I never criticized a jury in my 40-whatever years as solicitor and I'm not going to start now," he said. "But I would have done things differently if I was on that jury."

At the conclusion of a death-penalty trial in Walterboro, Murdaugh told the jurors that if they failed to find the accused guilty, a billboard should be erected on Interstate Highway 95 saying: "Murderers Welcome in Colleton County." Buster was sanctioned by the judge for this suggestion. The jury rendered a guilty verdict anyway.

Most folks assumed Murdaugh possessed vast knowledge of the law, but legal scholars and higher court judges knew better, often citing him for violating courtroom procedure and basic principles of law. But Buster played by his own rules and was greatly admired locally for it. He cared little about subsequent appeals, overturned verdicts and harsh media coverage. A local town police chief who was getting bad press once asked Murdaugh how he should respond. Simply laugh it off, Buster advised: "You can't out-piss a pole cat, and you can't out-print the press."

In his long career as the circuit solicitor, Murdaugh prosecuted 19 people who were executed after being strapped into "Old Sparky" — the nickname for South Carolina's long-venerated electric chair in Columbia. After retiring as solicitor, Buster told *The State* newspaper, "My job was over when the jury convicted them," adding he had never witnessed an electrocution. "I hear it's a pretty gruesome thing."

11

'BIG RED'

"Empires are not brought down by outside forces;
they are destroyed by weaknesses from within."
— Lionel Luther, TV character, "Smallville, USA"

For more than 80 years, the Randolph Murdaugh trilogy of solicitors grew the family's wealth, political power and social standing, all the while fending off nasty rumors and various threats, including a few minor criminal charges against them.

Buster's son, Randolph (Handsome) III, had married Elizabeth (Libby) Alexander, a public school teacher and later a member of the Hampton County school board. Their first son was Randolph (Randy) Murdaugh IV, who joined the family firm after graduating from the University of South Carolina, as did his younger brother Richard (Alex or Alec) Alexander Murdaugh — nicknamed "Big Red" because he was more than six feet tall with scarlet hair. Randolph and Libby also had a daughter, Lynn, and their youngest son, John Marvin, neither of whom became lawyers. The family lived in a large house in The Pines neighborhood of Varnville.

Randolph III and Libby Murdaugh quickly immersed themselves socially and politically in Hampton and the other four counties of the 14th Judicial Circuit. Dr. James Tuten, a college history professor who now lives in Pennsylvania, grew up with the Murdaugh children in The Pines, which he facetiously described as "a rough neighborhood" because it included the homes of prominent lawyers, bankers and judges. Tuten and Alex started school together at Jack-in-the-Box Kindergarten and they graduated from Wade Hampton High School in 1986.

"Alec had a big personality ... all those Murdaughs do. He was high energy, kind of loud, always the center of attention," Tuten recalled, adding his classmate's personality changed depending on whom he was around. Alex focused his attention on the most popular, prettiest girls at school. He was elected Prom King as an upperclassman and voted "Wittiest, Best All Around and Most Athletic" his senior year. He was tall and athletic, a three-sport letterman in high school — most notably as an offensive tight end on the Red Devil football team. In the yearbook he is pictured in his red football jersey with a cute girl at his side.

It was an age in Hampton County when corporal punishment in school for misbehaving boys was administered by grown men wielding wooden paddles. Tuten remembers when he, Alex and two other high school class-mates broke some rules and were summoned to Coach Phil Strother's office. Strother knew how to wield a paddle. The boys accepted their fates while Alex pleaded his case.

"Right away," Tuten said, "Alex tried to persuade Coach Strother not to paddle us, saying, 'Come on, coach,' and putting on a show … mostly for laughs. Even the coach laughed a little before giving Alex his first lick … When Alex pleaded his case again, I knew he was going to be a lawyer. The verdict had come down, still he was doing his best to get a different one or have his sentence commuted."

Throughout high school, Alex maintained his status as a member of the so-called "in crowd." "His last name got him that," said Ginger Harriot Hadwin, who also went to Wade Hampton High. Everybody knew who Alex was, she said, adding he was quietly criticized by some of his peers. Ginger's older sister was Gloria Harriot Satterfield, who years later fell down the front steps while working at Murdaugh's hunting estate Moselle and died of her injuries.

Another schoolmate, who asked not to be identified, described Alex as unchained, with no sense of being held accountable for anything. Others said he treated those he considered his equals in one way and was less respectful of those he considered beneath his elite status. After his wife and young-est son died at Moselle in 2019, an October 2020 article in *The Guardian* newspaper of London quoted unidentified classmates who described Alex as a bully who abused lower-class kids.

Ginger Hadwin remembers an incident involving Alex at the Varnville Pool and pavilion, a popular party spot where generations of teens and young adults enjoyed live bands, danced and socialized. She said Alex, who had been drinking, tried to pick a fight with her brother Eric. "Alex was a hot head," she said.

The old and beloved Varnville pool was on S.C. Highway 68 about two miles from the Murdaugh family homeplace at Almeda. Alex's grandparents, Gladys and Buster Murdaugh Jr., had moved their entire house from Carolina Avenue in Varnville up the tracks and placed it at the original homestead near where Grays Highway (U.S. 278) to Hilton Head Island merges with S.C. Highway 68 west of Yemassee. After Buster and Gladys Murdaugh passed away, Randolph III and Libby moved into the Almeda house.

As Alex and his brothers got older, they hosted parties in a field behind his grandfather's house — typically on Friday nights after high school football games. The Murdaugh boys provided kegs of beer, bonfires and the music. It soon became the scene of underage drinking and backseat romances. On occasion, whiffs of marijuana smoke were in the air. The partygoers didn't worry about getting DUI tickets when returning home from a bash at Almeda. Police seldom stopped kids who had been at the Murdaugh place.

The Guardian of London quoted Suzy Murdaugh, described as a relative from the less affluent side of the family, as saying Alex was a "full-blown alcoholic" back then, adding, "three earlier generations of the Murdaughs ran moonshine … We come from a long line of alcoholics."

Alex was the fourth Murdaugh to play football for the University of South Carolina Gamecocks, and later both he and his brother Randy were the fourth generation of Murdaugh men who practiced law in the family firm. In addition, Alex was the fourth generation of Murdaugh lawyers to serve the 14th Circuit Solicitor's Office, albeit as a part-time assistant prosecutor.

Alex received a bachelor's degree from the University of South Carolina in political science in 1990 and his juris doctorate from the USC law school. In November 1994 he was admitted to the Hampton County, the South Carolina and the American bar associations. He was also a member of the S.C. Association of Justice and the American Association of Justice. He worked briefly with his college roommate, Cory Fleming, at the Moss, Kuhn & Fleming law firm in Beaufort before joining the Murdaugh family practice in Hampton.

Alex and Maggie Kennedy Branstetter met in Columbia when they were USC undergraduates. They married in 1993 while Alex was in law school. They named their first child Richard Alexander Murdaugh Jr., born in 1996 and called "Buster" in honor of his great-grandfather. His brother, Paul, arrived three years later.

After his stint in the Beaufort law firm Alex and family moved to Hampton, where he soon became a partner in what by then was known as the PMPED (Peters, Murdaugh, Parker, Eltzroth and Detrick) law firm. He worked with his father, Randolph III, as a volunteer assistant solicitor, and also handled personal injury cases in both state and federal courts. Those cases involved victims of lucrative product liability and trip-and-fall incidents in big-box stores, vehicle and tire-defect lawsuits, and wrongful deaths. He won one case that involved a teenager about to start college who was seriously injured in a 2018 boating accident in the Savannah River near Allendale. Alex handled that case one year before his son Paul was involved in the boat crash that killed Mallory Beach.

Throughout his career Alex followed the Murdaugh playbook. He was active in legal, political and community circles. He served on the boards of a small college and a community endowment fund. He was a member of the Hampton County chapter of the NAACP. He also served for years as chairman of the local Democratic Party.

Alex and other family members were generous political donors, together giving more than $110,000 to South Carolina politicians in the most recent decade. The PMPED law firm's donations nearly doubled that. Alex donated to a variety of state politicians, town council members and local sheriffs — both Democrat and Republican. He backed S.C. Gov. Henry McMaster, 14th Circuit Solicitor Duffie Stone and S.C. Sen. Richard Harpootlian, a criminal defense lawyer he hired to represent Paul in the fatal boat crash. Alex was by far the biggest political donor in his family, doling out more than $90,000 to politicians from 2008 to 2020 while reporting the gifts under various versions of his name. Records on the state ethics website list him donating money as Richard, Richard Alexander, R. Alexander, Alexander and Alex Murdaugh — all of which was legal. But the gifts were generally considered to be attempts to purchase power, influence and access to state and local officials.

For years Alex Murdaugh lived a sun-soaked, sportsman's lifestyle in South Carolina's Lowcountry. He hunted and fished, and with his family seemed to enjoy boating, golfing, attending oyster roasts, fancy dinners and formal balls. He owned at least five boats, a house on Edisto Beach, and shares in three wooded tracts and seven islands in Beaufort County. His family owned a river house near the Broad River at a place called Murdaugh Island. Alex was also a member of and shareholder of the Green Swamp Club in Tillman, near Ridgeland, S.C.

Alex and his family lived in a rambling house at 515 Holly St. Extension in Hampton before moving to Moselle, the 1,770-acre hunting estate on the Big Salkehatchie River and straddling the Hampton/Colleton county line. The Moselle house is at the end of a tree-lined main avenue not far from an old airstrip and hangar, and dog kennels. The Murdaughs employed housekeepers and others to clean the home, wash and iron clothes, prepare meals, tend to the dogs and maintain wildlife food plots on the property.

Alex, his sons and friends used thermal (night-hunting) scopes and semi-automatic rifles to kill wild hogs. Low areas were planted and flooded to attract waterfowl. Organized dove, duck, turkey and deer hunts were popular at Moselle among Alex's family, friends, allies, clients and state game wardens. The walk-in coolers were always stocked with beer. However, Moselle was also like a house of cards, and the ground was shaking.

12

MOONSHINE CONSPIRACIES

*"You can't out-piss a pole cat, and you can't out-print the press
... So, if y'all think you can get rid of ol' Buster, you've got
another 'think' coming."*
— Randolph "Buster" Murdaugh

The following story is either untrue or highly exaggerated:

Solicitor Randolph Murdaugh Jr. lost what he thought would be a slam-dunk bestiality case against a man caught in the act with a goat. The accused took the stand and claimed he was a victim of entrapment.

"Are you saying the goat seduced you?" Buster asked.

"Well," the man said, "that nanny goat backed her rear end right up to the fence and enticed me."

Buster knew he lost the case when one farmer on the jury turned to another and said, "A good goat will do that, you know."

Ask around about Alex Murdaugh's grandfather and you'll likely get two answers: Buster was a legendary prosecutor who helped good people and put away bad ones, or Buster was a legendary crook and proverbial snake in the grass. There's truth in both points of view. Randolph "Buster" Murdaugh Jr. was a complicated man.

His legacy loomed large on both sides of South Carolina's legal system — one of prosecuting criminals in the people's name, the other defending ordinary folks victimized by large, faceless entities (railroad companies, for instance) with deep pockets. Buster was a charmer. Everyone knew that "the law" was in his corner of the courtroom. He inherited his father's abundant ambition and spent 45 years building the Murdaugh legal dynasty.

As the seldom challenged chief prosecutor for the 14th Circuit, Buster worked hard to maintain his voter base while wooing public officials and law enforcement officers alike. As a personal-injury lawyer, he won multi-million-dollar verdicts for thousands of "little guys," and everyone, including the highly paid attorneys who faced him in court, knew it. That's one reason his high-dollar settlements were common. His ability to get friendly judges on the bench was another. A May 1975 editorial in *The State* newspaper questioned the selection process for several circuit judges, and surely got Murdaugh's attention. It noted that "old-time political cronyism" had landed a judgeship for Clyde A. Eltzroth, a former state representative of Hampton and partner in the Murdaugh law firm. Eltzroth didn't have a law degree, or any college degree for that matter. He simply "read the law" under Buster Murdaugh, an apprenticeship allowed at the time.

Eltzroth had served on the Hampton County Democratic Party's executive committee from 1948 to 1960, and in the state House of Representatives from 1960-64. He was elected a circuit judge by the S.C. General Assembly, even though one of his opponents was endorsed by five county bar associations — two of them in the 14th Circuit. Solicitor Murdaugh was delighted when Eltzroth became a judge. Buster continued to prosecute almost all major criminal cases in his circuit singlehanded or later with his son, Randolph Murdaugh III.

All the while, Buster was criticized by newspaper editors and others for ethical issues and a few alleged criminal activities. Newspapers regaled readers well into the 1960s with stories of one accusation after another about him. But nothing stuck. Every four years, 14th Circuit voters re-elected Buster Murdaugh as their solicitor.

Controversy dogged Buster's legal career from the start. He was accused of tax evasion, stealing from clients, conspiring to break state and federal laws, taking bribes, and witness and jury tampering. Among the oddest allegations was he had stolen a Bluffton woman's cows. In September 1947, Buster received a letter threatening legal action from a former client, Ruth Vaux Cram, about legal fees and other matters. But Murdaugh sued her first, claiming she owed him money for handling her marriage separation, alimony payments and other legal work. He told a newspaper reporter she was a wealthy Northern woman who had married local millionaire Henry S. "Harry" Cram. Buster said he spent much time, travel and expense helping her on a number of legal matters, including her discharge from the Navy. He said he assisted her with investments, and was owed fees for that too.

..... Cram quickly filed an answer as well as two counter-claims alleging ...urdaugh had withheld money meant for her that he had received from her husband. She also said Buster had not acted in her best interest with her own investments. She said Murdaugh "made a studied effort to find out what investments (she) had, and a studied effort to get his hands on (her) investments and securities."

Mrs. Cram's most interesting allegation involved $20,000 she said Murdaugh owed her for a missing herd of her cows. She said she left her husband's Foot-Point Plantation but had no place to keep her 21 cows. Murdaugh told her he had a suitable place near Varnville for the animals, she said, and promised to care for the cows until she sold them. She said she had agreed to give him one cow for his troubles. But when she sent cattle buyers to get the other 20 cows, one of Murdaugh's employees told them they were being held for unpaid fees.

Buster's counterclaim included "wordage that would smoke up asbestos paper," according to an article in Charleston's *News and Courier*. Murdaugh claimed the cows arrived at his farm without his prior knowledge, that he told Mrs. Cram he could not care for them, and had objected to her animals being there. Buster said he and members of his office staff repeatedly asked her to remove the cows because they were unruly, and wandered onto his neighbors' property and destroyed crops, losses for which he had to pay. He said the cows were diseased and had infected his own cattle, and that all but one of Mrs. Cram's cows had died. The lone survivor was sold to cover his veterinarian bills, Buster said.

Murdaugh was represented in that case by Allendale lawyer Thomas M. Boulware, who asked that it be transferred from Hampton County to a court in St. Matthews in Calhoun County after two 14th Circuit District judges were disqualified from hearing the matter. One judge recused himself, citing a long friendship with Murdaugh, and the other would be called to testify on Buster's behalf if the case came to trial. A hearing scheduled in St. Matthews was canceled at the last minute after Boulware and Cram's attorney, Hugh O. Hanna, settled the case. The terms were never made public.

Despite the back-and-forth drama involving "wild and unruly" disease-spreading bovines, Murdaugh, when asked for a comment by *The Hampton County Guardian,* said there was "nothing unusual about the matter at all," adding the only dispute was about his fee. "Frankly, an attempt is being made to make much ado about nothing, and, of course, being in politics my political enemies apparently are attempting to lower themselves and hurt me by spreading malicious rumors, and by requesting that statements of this case be printed."

Six months later the Hampton County Bar Association asked the S.C. Bar's grievance committee for a full investigation of the way Murdaugh had treated another one of his clients. J.V. McMillan of Hampton County had filed a $50,000 breach-of-trust suit against Murdaugh and also asked that Buster be disbarred. Murdaugh had obtained money from McMillian to pay off a mortgage, the suit alleged, but Buster never did. Murdaugh denied any wrongdoing, saying the accusation was politically motivated. "It has always been my policy to fight my politics at the polls, but it would appear there are others who prefer to employ different means in such matters," he told a reporter. "I take it that those who wish to injure me want to try their cases in the press."

Later, after what one newspaper described as a secret investigation and another as a secret hearing, Buster was cleared by the S.C. Bar Association. Murdaugh then filed a countersuit claiming McMillan owed him $825, and publicly criticized the man for wasting the county's resources on a frivolous suit against a well-respected solicitor. "It is regrettable that the cost of this investigation, in the payment of witnesses' expenses and the serving of sub-poenas, will have to be borne by the taxpayers of Hampton County ... and I estimate it will run well over a thousand dollars," he told the press.

In 1955 the Internal Revenue Service charged Murdaugh with tax fraud for under-reporting his income. The IRS alleged that he owed nearly $16,000 in back taxes for the years 1945-48, plus more than $7,000 in penalties. Buster said it was a misunderstanding that resulted from poor recordkeeping, and was cleared of criminal wrongdoing. "It may be that the petitioner was 'grossly negligent' in the keeping of records for tax purposes," the appeals judge said, "so much he (Murdaugh) virtually concedes. But however much his method of keeping records and assembling information for his tax returns left to be desired, carelessness is not synonymous with fraud."

In October 1968, Murdaugh was charged with "larceny after trust with fraudulent intent" in connection with a sawmill sale four years earlier. The warrant was signed by L.J. Williams of Yemassee on behalf of his wife, who owned Varnville Wood Products Company. Williams alleged that Murdaugh, who was his business partner, oversaw the sale and the transfer of the title to the sawmill. Williams claimed the mill sold for $22,000 — $15,000 more than he had invested — but that Buster kept the profit, which was supposed to split between partners.

In court Williams produced a deed showing the sale of the sawmill to Hampton County Wood Products, Inc. Buster's attorneys, however, argued that their client never got his share of the profits. They introduced papers showing a judgement had been placed against the sawmill for the sale amount because Buster had never been paid. After a three-hour hearing, the Hampton County magistrate dismissed the charges, saying that there was insufficient cause to bring a case.

As Murdaugh consolidated his power and weathered storms of controversy, Martha Bee Anderson rose through the ranks of South Carolina's male-dominated journalism as a writer for *The State* newspaper in Columbia and *The News and Courier* in Charleston before becoming the editor of the weekly *Hampton County Guardian*. Martha Bee — blonde, of Scandinavian descent, rather short in height and often seen riding a bicycle around town — looked more like a kindly kindergarten teacher than Buster's fearless nemesis. She enjoyed gathering news and social chatter for the local paper while stopping here and there to pick up roadside litter in her quest to clean up her beloved Hampton. Inside her Viking chest beat the heart of a courageous journalist who covered everything from rural health-care problems and environmental degradation to horrible crimes and local corruption.

Her son, Carl Anderson, a retired surgeon living in Greenville, recalls being the only child of the small-town South Carolina newspaper editor. He said his mother took him with her on assignments, which included covering a Ku Klux Klan rally and a nighttime raid on a moonshine operation. During the raid he saw two scruffy men handcuffed in the back of a police car as hounds bayed into the distance on the scents of others. Bags of sugar and barrels of home-made liquor were everywhere. Martha Bee joked about grabbing a bag of sugar to bake a cake later.

Dr. Anderson also remembered the Murdaughs and their law firm. "I don't know how much she knew about the Murdaugh outfit back then, but I do know she did not respect Buster much at all. A lot of people were intimidated by him." He said his mother seemed hesitant at times to write stories critical of Buster Murdaugh because of the power he wielded in the community.

But she went after him anyway for 20 years in the pages of *The Hampton County Guardian*. She reported on a variety of scandals and legal wrangles in which the solicitor and his law firm were involved. She had earned her statewide reputation as a newswoman who told it like it was.

In 1963 she paid particular attention to an adoption scandal in Jasper County in which Ridgeland lawyer Delmar "Tiny" Rivers, who had served in the S.C. House of Representatives, was accused of forging a circuit judge's name to a dozen sets of adoption papers, and reportedly forging Buster's name to six more. While a grand jury declined to indict Rivers, he was disbarred by the S.C. Supreme Court in 1965. The fact that Solicitor Murdaugh was involved had local folks talking, and Martha Bee Anderson was one of them, recalled her son.

Buster liked to brag about winning numerous convictions as a prosecutor. However, it was not unusual for his wins to be overturned because he had in some manner threatened juries who disagreed with him. In 1961 the state Supreme Court overturned a death-penalty conviction of accused rapist Fred G. Davis, a Marine Corps private who admitted to police that he had overpowering sex urges and enjoyed using force on women. The high court rebuked Solicitor Murdaugh because he told the jurors that if they did not convict Davis, a white man accused of raping a black woman, he would "turn loose" a black man charged with raping a white woman in an upcoming death-penalty trial. Buster declined to prosecute Davis the second time. Davis was later acquitted by an all-white, male jury.

In May 1981 the state Supreme Court overturned Solicitor Murdaugh's death penalty conviction of Michael Linder for murdering S.C. Highway Patrolman Willie Peeples in Colleton County. The high court ordered the case re-tried, partly because of errors in the judge's instructions to the jury and partly because of Murdaugh's comments in his closing arguments: "If you don't find him (Linder) guilty, we should put up a sign in blood on Interstate 95 saying 'Murderers Welcome in Colleton County'." The justices' ruling stated, "We admonish the solicitor... his argument must be carefully tailored so as not to appeal to the personal bias of the juror nor be calculated to arouse his passion or prejudice." Linder was retried and acquitted in November 1981.

A month earlier, cases against three Death Row inmates prosecuted by Murdaugh were also overturned. The S.C. Supreme Court cited five major errors in the first trial of Sylvester Lewis Adams of Rock Hill, S.C., who was charged with kidnapping and murdering a teenager in Beaufort County. Adams was again convicted, then executed by lethal injection in August 1995 despite his attorneys' objections about his mental status.

The court upheld the convictions but overturned death sentences for John David Arnold and John H. Plath for the brutal 1978 rape and killing of the black woman who had hitched a ride in Beaufort County. The state ordered a new trial to determine if the men should receive life imprisonment or death based on Murdaugh's conduct during the trial. The justices stated that Murdaugh erred when he told the jury he would never ask for the death penalty in Beaufort again if the jury did not order the men's executions. After their second trial both men were returned to Death Row and executed in 1998.

In November 1981, the state Supreme Court overturned the death sentence for Ronald Raymond "Rusty" Woomer, citing "unfair cross-examination" by Solicitor Murdaugh during his 1980 trial for murder and armed robbery. Woomer was described in an Associated Press article as a "thief who went on a murderous rampage that left four people dead and another maimed for life." After a second trial, Woomer was again sentenced to death and executed in 1990.

By far the biggest blemish on Murdaugh's record occurred when he was accused by federal agents of taking part in a case dubbed by the press as "The Great Colleton County Whiskey Conspiracy," which engulfed local law enforcement officers, magistrates and the chief prosecutor himself. The scandal was "born in violence on a cold November morning" in 1951, according to *The State* newspaper, when federal agent Henderson Clary shot and wounded Colleton County bootlegger D.B "Doc" Freeman, who unbeknownst to the feds, was "in cahoots" with local lawmen and court officials and didn't take kindly to being shot by men he thought were on his side.

After a five-year investigation, Solicitor Murdaugh was one of 30 people indicted by federal grand juries in Columbia and Charleston for conspiracy to violate Internal Revenue Service laws regarding liquor sales. Also indicted was Colleton County Sheriff G. Haskell Thompson, who the governor promptly ordered removed from office. Thompson refused to turn in his badge. The sheriff appealed to the S.C. Supreme Court, which refused to hear it. Thompson lost his re-election bid in the June 12, 1955 Democratic primary.

Murdaugh, meanwhile, was accused of conspiring with others to obtain from bootlegger Doc Freeman's wife, Edith, a notebook documenting her husband's protection payments to local authorities. Buster was also accused of conspiring to relocate an illegal distillery prior to an upcoming police raid. Buster allegedly had warned Robert F. Clifton to move his liquor still from Hampton County to Colleton County. Buster posted bond and got a short delay ostensibly because he was busy prosecuting cases in Beaufort. The case was scheduled for trial in federal district court in Charleston and prosecutors planned to call as many as a thousand witnesses.

Buster's defense attorneys, Henry H. Edens and Henry Hammer, filed motions to either dismiss the charges or try Murdaugh separately from the others. Among the grounds for doing so were allegations that federal prosecutors promised Buster's fellow defendants light sentences in exchange for damaging testimony against the solicitor. His lawyers noted that Buster had prosecuted many of the co-conspirators, thus his "substantial rights to a fair trial will be prejudiced." U.S. Judge Walter E. Hoffman denied motions to dismiss Murdaugh's indictments altogether, denied the request for a separate trial for the solicitor and refused to strike three "overt acts" in which Murdaugh was charged.

Judge Hoffman later ordered federal prosecutors to turn over a list of all witnesses to Murdaugh's defense counsel, and to provide a list of documentary evidence. The release of witness names proved problematic for federal prosecutors. A U.S. Department of Justice memo issued after the trial had stated that the disclosure resulted in "very questionable practices on the part of some of the defendants and their attorneys during which government witnesses were threatened, attempts were made to influence them by promises of reward for themselves or for members of their families, and at least one attempt was made to intimidate or influence the United States Attorney."

Why did the governor order removal of the Colleton County sheriff from his elected post but take no such action against Solicitor Murdaugh? That was a question posed in a *Greenville News* article under the headline: "Solicitor To Be Tried in One Court, Prosecute in Another Same Time."

Indeed, Buster Murdaugh was slated to prosecute cases in General Sessions Court in Walterboro while at the same time answering charges against himself in the U.S. Courthouse in Charleston for his role in the whiskey conspiracy. When a circuit solicitor is unable to prosecute a case in his own district, the state's attorney general is supposed to appoint a prosecutor from another circuit as a replacement. However, Attorney General T.C. Callison told the newspaper he had not received a request to replace Solicitor Murdaugh.

"Unless there is a change somewhere, 14th Circuit Solicitor Randolph Murdaugh of Hampton will have to be in two courts at once on Sept. 17, as prosecutor in one and defendant in the other," the *Greenville News* reported. But on Sept. 6, Buster voluntarily resigned as solicitor to devote all his time to preparing for his own defense in a federal criminal trial expected to last up to six weeks. Murdaugh also wrote to S.C. Gov. George Timmerman Jr. that he was innocent of all charges levied as a "result of the activities of certain federal agents."

"The security, honor and happiness of my wife and children face destruction; my personal integrity and liberty are at stake," he wrote. He also expressed his appreciation for Gov. Timmerman's "confidence in my integrity" and said that he welcomed an early opportunity to clear his name of the "outrageous charges." His letter concluded: "With the help of Almighty God, the falsity of the charges will be bared and I will return to the office of Solicitor." Gov. Timmerman accepted his resignation the same day and appointed Beaufort lawyer G.G. Dowling as his interim replacement.

On the first day of the trial, Doc Freeman's wife testified she handled payoffs from bootleggers to law enforcement officials. She also said $13,000 in cash had disappeared from her house during the Nov. 15, 1951 liquor raid during which her husband was shot. She said deputies searched the house and the "bundle of money" disappeared. The crooked cops later gave her $500 and her husband $2,000, she said.

In cross-examination by Murdaugh's defense lawyers, Mrs. Freeman said the bundle of money was stolen from the pocket of a coat hanging in a closet at her house. "I do think Sheriff Thompson, Mr. Murdaugh and [Deputy] Lucas Hiott got the money, but I can't prove it," she testified.

Other witnesses testified about being paid to work liquor stills owned by police officers, and in order to operate their own stills, paid the sheriff with cases of moonshine and cash. The money was often divided among cronies who included deputies, magistrates and the solicitor, according to testimony. Former bootlegger Joe T. Padgett of Beaufort testified he got into the illegal whiskey business in Colleton County in 1952. Padgett said a co-defendant, Colleton Magistrate Berkeley C. Wood, had introduced him to Sheriff Thompson to discuss purchasing protection payments. "The sheriff asked me how much I could pay a month, and I told him $200," Padgett said. "He told me to go ahead and get a location." Padgett said he gave 12 cases of moonshine a month to Sheriff Thompson and Magistrate Wood. "Thompson told me if I could get $200 — that was $100 for him and $100 for Mr. Murdaugh — he would see what he could do" to get light probationary sentences for two of Padgett's helpers, who also had been arrested.

Ex-Colleton Deputy Sheriff Ribbock Herndon testified that he gave Thompson $400 monthly in cash from retail stores and in bootlegger payoffs. He also said he sold whiskey, kept 20 percent for himself and gave the rest to the sheriff. Herndon said he once gave Thompson four $100 bills from whiskey payouts while inside the Colleton courthouse, then saw Thompson give two of the bills to Murdaugh. Buster got very angry because the money was exchanged in Herndon's presence, the ex-deputy said.

During the second week of the trail, Buster reportedly took the stand and a heated "parry-and-thrust battle of wits and tempers" followed between the solicitor and assistant U.S. Attorney Irvine Belser Jr. Judge Hoffman warned both men to calm down before threatening to charge Belser with contempt of court.

The defense called several character witnesses in support of Buster, including Hampton County grain elevator owner/operator Grover C. Bowers, of Estill. Bowers described Murdaugh as a man of very good character. In response, the federal prosecutor introduced four character witnesses who testified against Murdaugh's "reputation for truth and veracity," according to newspaper coverage.

In final rounds of questioning, Belser got Buster to confirm a statement that the Murdaugh law firm had been paid $1,733 by one of the witnesses, bootlegger Robert Clifton, for handling a previous whiskey case that went all the way to the U.S. Supreme Court. All of which did not appear to sit well with Judge Hoffman.

Final arguments began on Sept. 28 and the matter was set to go to the jury on Saturday, Sept. 29. The jury asked the judge to wait until Monday. Judge Hoffman agreed, and urged the jurors to refrain from reading newspapers over the weekend.

On Monday during final arguments, the assistant district attorney described the indicted public officials, including Buster, as "a bunch of buzzards and vultures." Murdaugh defense attorney Claud N. Sapp described the government witnesses as "a bunch of perjurers, thieves and convicts."

Judge Hoffman advised the jury that it must reach a verdict and he would send them back repeatedly until it did. "This case is too complicated and lengthy to face a second hearing." The verdict soon followed. Murdaugh and two other defendants were acquitted of all charges. Charges against four other defendants were dismissed. Five of the accused had changed their pleas to guilty early in the trial in exchange for lighter sentences. The remaining 17 defendants included the recently defeated sheriff, two of his deputies and the former magistrate. One defendant, Harry Richards, was missing. The sheriff was sentenced to seven years in prison and a $3,000 fine. The deputies and magistrate received three-year sentences, and the others got two years or less.

In the final day of the session, as he was hearing pleas for leniency for the convicted, Judge Hoffman harshly criticized the acquitted, including Solicitor Murdaugh. The judge described Buster's conduct as being grossly unethical, including the fact that the solicitor had represented accused bootleggers in previous federal proceedings.

"I can't get involved in Colleton County politics, but I notice by the newspapers that Mr. Murdaugh plans to go back into office as solicitor," Judge Hoffman said. "He is an acquitted man and that is his prerogative. However, his unethical conduct — so grossly unethical by his own admission — was such that I couldn't go back and face my people if I were he. But that's his business and the business of the people there."

Neither Buster nor his attorneys were in court that day. Murdaugh later described the judge's damning words as an attack on him. "It was unwarranted and entirely uncalled for in every respect … Because the judge's comments are privileged, having been made in open court, I have no recourse." He did say his representation of bootleggers in federal court was a long-standing practice in South Carolina authorized by state law. "When the federal government sends a Republican judge into this state to tell South Carolinians how to handle their politics, it's a perfect example of the further encroachment by the government on the rights of the state."

A November 1956 memo by the U.S. Department of Justice about the trial further condemned Murdaugh: "The defense resorted to some highly questionable tactics, all apparently designed to bring about an acquittal or mistrial as to Solicitor Murdaugh even at the risk of sacrificing the remaining defendants. Strange incidents occurred during the trial, which sorely taxed the patience of the prosecutor. At one time one of the government's principal witnesses, after having testified previously in court, came to the United States Attorney and told him that he had lied on the stand. Brought before the Court, however, he would admit only that his testimony had been erroneous in certain very immaterial respects which did not affect the issues in the case. Oddly enough, too, the foreman of the jury, immediately before the case was to go to the jury for deliberation, having received a telephone call informing him that his father was dying, declined to accept the court's proffer of release, although an alternate juror was still present and available to take the foreman's place. It has been admitted by the foreman that he attended school with a brother of the defendant Murdaugh and in fact had dinner with him shortly before the trial began.

"As result of this case, two obstruction of justice indictments have been returned and other allegations of misconduct with respect to the government's witnesses are under investigation. Although acquitted, Solicitor Murdaugh was publicly castigated for his unethical practices by Judge Walter Hoffman … The Judge also felt it necessary publicly to call attention to the fact that it is a separate and distinct offense for anyone to threaten a person who has testified in court proceedings."

Rebecca Hill, who was elected Colleton County's Clerk of Court in 2020, had older relatives who were swept up in the county's whiskey ring controversy. She said her grandfather, Felder Hiers, faced charges as part of the combined federal and local investigation when a liquor still on his farm on Henderson Highway was raided. Like many others, the Hiers family had a history of making moonshine and of enjoying consumption their product.

When the final verdicts were read, Hiers family members and other Colleton County residents didn't take kindly to serving time in prison while Buster Murdaugh was not punished, Hill said. "I remember them saying how unfair it was that the person in charge of all of this got off scot-free while the minor people went to prison. Fortunately, they got minor sentences, and the liquor stills were back up and running at some point … a lot of people in town looked down on my granddaddy for what happened." She said one of her relatives, who helped make illegal liquor but was not arrested because he was a minor, later wanted to date a local girl. When her parents found out she was being courted by a member of a known bootlegging family, they refused to let her see him. So they courted secretly and eventually married.

"True love found its way," Hill said.

Indeed, love is strange. Federal officials could say what they wanted to about Buster Murdaugh, but he had the love and loyalty of most voters in the 14th Circuit. His supporters included members of the Hampton County grand jury. In an Oct. 10, 1956, statement to *The Hampton County Guardian*, the grand jury commended Buster "for the splendid manner in which he has handled the affairs of the office of solicitor. We deplore the outrageous charges brought against him and rejoice in his vindication. We sincerely hope he will return to the office of solicitor in the very near future and will continue to serve in that office as long as he desires ..."

On Nov. 6, 1956, Murdaugh was swept back into office by a sizable majority of voters in all five counties in the circuit, and on Nov. 19 the governor officially returned the solicitor to his post.

In the September 1957 term of Colleton County General Sessions, Murdaugh got revenge against two of the witnesses and co-conspirators who had testified against him in exchange for lesser or dismissed charges. The solicitor pressed state charges against former deputy Riddick H. Herndon, a primary federal witness in the conspiracy trial, and former Jacksonboro district magistrate Herman M. Tuten for violations of the state's liquor laws as part of the Colleton whiskey ring. They were accused of the same crimes they had faced in the federal trial. Both men pleaded no contest to the state charges.

13

RUMORS

Afunctioning grist mill is hard to find around here anymore. But the small-town rumor mill still grinds out tons of gossip: Who stole what? Who's sleeping with whom? Who is the baby's real father? Scuttlebutt scurries along the grapevine in giggles and groans and grave expressions of shock. Wrap a powerful family name like Murdaugh around the tale, the harder it is to separate fiction from fact.

That's what began on July 8, 2015 when a dead man was found in the pre-dawn darkness sprawled across the middle of a seldom traveled, two-lane highway not far from town. The body of Stephen Smith, 19, a local man, was spotted at 4 a.m. by a passerby on his way to work. He called 911. What happened next is all rather curious. Rumor had it that Alex and Maggie Murdaugh's sons were involved.

Smith's skull was smashed, he had injuries on his left arm and hand — as if he had tried to defend himself — and his body was faceup on the highway in a bloody pool near the yellow centerline. His shoes were loosely tied and still on his feet. No skid marks, debris or other signs of a vehicle were found. Perhaps he was hit by a wide side mirror of a passing truck. But if so, why didn't he see headlights or hear the truck coming, and get off the road? Was he killed elsewhere and placed on the highway to make it look like an accident?

The investigation passed like a game of tag from one law enforcement agency to another. Hampton County sheriff's deputies were among the first to arrive at the scene and the county coroner was notified. At first it appeared as if Smith had been shot in the head, so State Law Enforcement Division crime-team investigators were summoned from Columbia. After a cursory check of the body and the scene, SLED turned the case over to the S.C. Highway Patrol, whose officers are trained to investigate traffic accidents and routine fatalities.

But nothing was routine about the death of the young man who was studying to become a hospital nurse. Smith was homosexual, which was no secret among his former Wade Hampton High School classmates, and rumor had it he had been seeing one of the Murdaugh boys. Word of Smith's strange demise spread fast: *"The dead boy was gay, beaten to death with a baseball bat, and he knew the Murdaugh boys ..."*

Hampton's hometown newspaper rarely reported rumors. It's not good journalism and risky. Defending libel suits can be very expensive. But a rumor persisted about Stephen's death: A high school baseball game, or practice, occurred that night; an extended-cab pickup with a Carolina Gamecocks bumper sticker sped north through the darkness on Sandy Run Road; inside were four teen-age boys fueled by beer, raging hormones and homophobia; one brought along an aluminum baseball bat.

Authorities confirmed that Stephen was alone when his car apparently ran out of fuel in the vicinity of Sandy Run Road between the town of Hampton and Moselle, the Murdaugh hunting estate. They said his phone didn't work and noted that someone or something struck and killed him, then left the scene where the body was found.

Four months after Stephen's death, the editor of *The Hampton County Guardian* called the newspaper's lone reporter into his office, its walls cluttered with historical photos, journalism awards and his children's crayon drawings. Yellowing stacks of newspapers were everywhere. "Next week is Thanksgiving and families will gather at dining-room tables, count their blessings, express their gratitude," the editor said. "Do you know who won't be sitting at one of those tables?"

The reporter, a young Ohio transplant, nodded that he did. He was a country boy raised near the Kentucky line among guns, four-wheelers and homes of hard-working people like most folks who inhabit Hampton County.

"We're going with a story about Stephen Smith ..." the editor said, paused and looked his colleague in the eyes, " ... in our Thanksgiving edition, along with the warm and fuzzy crap we usually put in there. Call Stephen's mother. Ask her to come see us, that we need to run something that will strike a nerve of someone who knows something about what happened to her son."

The story was published on 1-A with a photo of Stephen and his mother, arms around each other and smiling. "I know who killed my son," Sandy Smith was quoted as saying, and alleged they included Stephen's former classmates from a prominent local family, which she declined to identify on record. A rare front-page editorial ran beside the story that was a plea for information to help solve the case: "It's time to do the right thing, Hampton County."

But those who actually knew what had happened were either afraid to say anything publicly or did not care. Weeks, months and years passed and no one was charged in the death of Stephen Smith. The rumors died down but the questions did not: Who killed Stephen Smith? Was he the victim of a hit-and-run driver and left for dead like so many deer killed at night in the Lowcountry? Was he murdered elsewhere and his body dumped like roadside litter? Would the truth ever be known?

In early February 2018, Gloria Satterfield, of the Furman community in Hampton County, tumbled down the front steps of the main house at Moselle, where she worked for Alex and Maggie Murdaugh. The long-time Murdaugh housekeeper had a serious head injury. She was hospitalized for 24 days and said very little before passing away.

Mrs. Satterfield, 57, was a widow and mother of two grown sons. After the fall, she was being treated for blood clotting and pneumonia when she suffered a heart attack, went into a coma and died. Maggie Murdaugh and son Paul were at Moselle when Gloria fell. Maggie called 911 and summoned help — all of which sparked more gossip about the Murdaugh family. Was Gloria's death accidental or was she pushed down the steps?

Alex Murdaugh claimed that, before the ambulance arrived, Gloria told him she had tripped over his pet dogs. Gloria's family questioned this because she had said nothing to anyone following the incident. Nevertheless, the Hampton County death certificate noted it was a "natural death." In reality, tripping over dogs might be accidental but certainly not natural.

Gloria's obituary in *The Hampton County Guardian* noted that she would be remembered for her laughter and outgoing personality, and listed her sons and other survivors as well as "those she loved as family," which was a reference to the Murdaughs, for whom she had worked for years. The funeral service was at Sandy Run Baptist Church, where Alex, Maggie and Paul were among mourners. Mrs. Satterfield had helped raise Paul, 18, at that time, and his brother, Buster, who is two years older. She was especially close to Paul.

After the service, most of the mourners filed out of the church and into their vehicles for the six-mile ride to Johnson-St. Paul Cemetery. Rural Southerners traditionally turn on their vehicle headlights while in route to a burial. Others driving on both sides of the road pull over and stop until the funeral procession passes. It's a matter of respect.

After the burial that day, mourners offered regrets to Gloria's sons and relatives, who represented the Satterfield, Harriott and Hadwin families, while members of the burial crew checked their watches and waited patiently. Alex Murdaugh spoke to Gloria's sons, Brian Harriott and Tony Satterfield: "Boys, this is my fault … all my fault … but I'm going to make this right." The sons glanced at each other, then at their uncles Scott and Eric Harriott, and back at the tall, well-dressed lawyer smiling through tobacco-stained teeth. "I'll file a lawsuit against my insurance company and get you boys some money," Alex said, and recommended Beaufort attorney Cory Fleming to handle the case. "Trust me!" he said.

14

FATHER AND SON TEAM

"My Daddy always said, 'I don't see anything wrong with nepotism, as long as you keep it in the family'."
— **Randolph Murdaugh III**

HAMPTON COUNTY —

Randolph "Buster" Murdaugh Jr. settled back in his leather chair, propped his feet on his desk and slowly unwrapped a cigar during an interview with a writer for the *Carolina Lawyer,* the University of South Carolina School of Law's journal.

Buster thrived on attention. His son, assistant solicitor Randolph III, sat dutifully nearby, as did his grandson Randolph IV, a second-year USC law student at the time. Buster pointed the unlit cigar toward Randolph III and said:

"I remember the time when I took that boy fishing. He couldn't have been more than seven or eight. We were sitting on the bank of the river when the sheriff came down to get us. They had recovered a body in a murder case and the victim's brother was in custody." The brother, a Colleton County farmer, had agreed to cooperate but would only talk to the solicitor. Anticipating a confession, Buster took his son along as a witness. At the jail the boy listened as the farmer told the solicitor that his semi-invalid sister, 80, had died and he buried her in the stable. Actually, her body was found in the hog pen. The grand jury indicted the farmer for murder "by starvation, poisoning or burying alive."

The trial was in the Colleton County Courthouse in Walterboro. Included on the witness list was the solicitor's young son, who had told his father he felt sorry for the farmer and did not want to testify. The solicitor said he must testify or he would declare the boy a hostile witness and he would have to sit in the courtroom with his subpoena in his hand.

"I didn't know what a subpoena was ... I thought it was something dirty," Randolph III smiled and said to the interviewer, adding that he did testify, the man was convicted of murdering his sister and sentenced to life in prison.

Buster told the interviewer that he, too, first learned about the law at his own father's knee. "I don't think it ever occurred to either one of us that I would be anything other than a lawyer."

Randolph Sr.'s earnings were lost during the Great Depression. He was broke when Buster got a full football scholarship to play at the University of South Carolina. Buster had several jobs in Columbia while he was in law school, working early on weekday mornings at the state highway department until his classes began at 9 a.m., and in the afternoons for the state insurance commission. When the Legislature was in session, Buster was a Senate clerk.

Randolph III said his father was hard-nosed when he had to be (Buster claimed he had sent 19 men to the electric chair). He said he was a good judge of character and had compassion for those he thought had redeeming values and came from good families.

Buster smiled when hearing his son's comments, then boasted about an informal pre-trial intervention program called "Solicitor's Probation," which he said he designed and administered to help people who had broken the law but deserved leniency. One man he had placed in the program became a successful Hampton County businessman who "every year at Christmas comes by my office to tell me how I changed his life," Buster told the interviewer.

Randolph III was born on Oct. 25, 1939, in Savannah, only a few months before his grandfather died in the train crash. As a child Randolph III accompanied his father at crime scenes, and was given the job of pulling juror numbers at courthouses throughout the district. After graduating from the University of South Carolina and earning his degree at the USC law school in 1964, he worked as his father's assistant solicitor until 1986, when Buster opted not to run again. Randolph III ran in his father's place, was elected solicitor and hired Buster for $8,000 annually as his deputy assistant primarily to help reduce the ever-growing caseload. There were times when Randolph III retried and won cases that previously were successfully prosecuted by his father and later were overturned, often because of Buster's courtroom antics and comments.

One murder case in the early 1970s, when Buster was solicitor and Randolph III was his assistant, stood out:

Wallace Youmans, an 18-year-old black man, died in a shotgun slaying in Fairfax, which straddles Hampton and Allendale counties, during a time when racial tension was running high in the area. Youmans was killed shortly after midnight as he walked along a highway. The murder was rumored to have been a reprisal for the wounding of a white man a week earlier. Civil rights leaders and others complained because state and local authorities had conducted a lengthy investigation but had not arrested anyone. They also accused Solicitor Murdaugh of not doing enough to bring the case to trial.

Years went by and still no one had been charged with killing Youmans. Civil rights leaders asked the FBI to investigate the case, and the U.S. Justice Department expressed interest in the outcome. Four years later an Allendale County grand jury finally took up the matter. They heard 25 hours of testimony from 35 witnesses and issued indictments charging five white men with the murder. They included Fairfax's long-time magistrate; a former town policeman; the owner of a nearby grocery store; and two others, all of whom reporters dubbed "The Fairfax Five."

That's when the state NAACP requested that S.C. Attorney General Daniel McLeod appoint a special prosecutor to replace Solicitor Murdaugh. McLeod declined to do that but did say he would assign state assistant attorneys to help Solicitor Murdaugh and his son prosecute the case.

Buster Murdaugh was not happy. "It seems right strange — and color doesn't mean anything to me — that a white man was shot at about the same time this (Youmans' murder) happened, but I've never seen one word printed about that. And I had not heard that anyone was trying to get me off this case," he told *The Hampton County Guardian.* "If you know who does, tell them to come to me and ask, and I'll gladly get off … But if they want a conviction in this case, they stand a better chance of getting one with me on it than if someone from the outside comes in because I know the people here. I know how they think."

Not long afterward, *The Guardian* reported that three witnesses, including a member of the local NAACP, admitted they were offered by an anonymous party a total of $1,500 to withhold certain testimony from the grand jury. The NAACP also claimed he had been harassed over the telephone by one of the accused men's relatives. Another witness told the local newspaper that a SLED captain had threatened to sue him if he "maligned the integrity" of the officer or the investigation. In addition, the Murdaughs alleged that SLED and local lawmen had withheld witnesses and evidence from the solicitor's office and the grand jury. Buster told *The Hampton County Guardian* he could "blow the lid off the Youmans' case" if they would cooperate.

That's when the FBI seized evidence the solicitor's office had not been able to obtain. It included tape recordings of police radio communications during two weekends of racial disturbances prior to the Youmans murder. The FBI also interviewed scores of witnesses on its own. A contentious evidence hearing followed. At the request of the Murdaughs and the state attorney general's office, new indictments for accessory and conspiracy charges were levied against two of the "The Fairfax Five."

The trial began that summer in the crowded Allendale County Courthouse, which had no air-conditioning. The Hampton and Allendale newspapers covered the trial and ran photos of Buster talking to witnesses at the crime scene, and Buster and Randolph III outside the courthouse. The jury heard testimony that at least two of the accused men had staked out the grocery store that night to defend it against vandalism, and the shooting occurred seconds after Youmans threw glass bottles that broke under the awning of the store. Two of the jurors told the judge that this testimony was in direct conflict with what they had previously been told by state and federal investigators.

Solicitor Murdaugh called two *Charlotte Observer* reporters to the stand to testify about the case because "they knew more than the federal and state investigators." Buster also advised the jury, "I know how you can stop this from happening again. If you'll find these two white men guilty of shooting this black man, you won't have any more of this kind of shooting in the county."

It wasn't until July 1974, after four days of testimony from more than 30 witnesses for both the prosecution and the defense, that the jury of seven blacks and five whites deliberated 80 minutes and delivered a verdict of not guilty for two of the accused. Later that day Solicitor Murdaugh announced he did not intend to prosecute the other three, and charges against them were withdrawn.

Buster told the press that the charges were dropped because he had no evidence to support the accusations against the other three and no evidence that they had conspired to commit a crime. One of three men whose charges were dropped was the Fairfax magistrate, who was reinstated.

In 1971 the S.C. General Assembly considered a bill that would pay solicitors for full-time jobs and prohibit them from practicing privately. Buster Murdaugh was the leader of the state solicitor's association at that time and spoke out against the proposal. He said his part-time state salary was only $22,000 a year, and he might have to retire if the measure passed. He also said he might stay if his full-time salary was commensurate with what the state's circuit judges were paid. The bill was signed into law, effective Jan. 1, 1977, and Buster stayed on as solicitor until he retired on Dec. 31, 1986.

Also in 1971, Solicitor Murdaugh was accused of nepotism for having his son, Randolph III, on the payroll. The Beaufort County Council complained about the family arrangement to Gov. James B. Edwards, the Beaufort County Legislative Delegation and the ethics committees of both the S.C. House and Senate. Randolph III had served unofficially in the solicitor's office starting in 1964. In 1969 Buster made his son's appointment official after telling the press he had offered the assistant solicitor job to several other lawyers, none of whom accepted. As an assistant, Randolph III was paid half his father's $20,000 salary plus $1,800 for expenses annually.

The State newspaper ran an editorial on Aug. 17, 1975 tagged "All in the Family," which noted that new 14th Circuit judge, Clyde A. Eltzroth, was Buster Murdaugh's long-time protégé and law partner, and described the 14th Circuit as having a worrisome "interlocking legal hierarchy." Members of the South Carolina Legislature said they took a hard look at nepotism laws as they applied to state governments, but offered no significant changes in the way the 14th Circuit Solicitor's Office was being run.

In April 1978, Solicitor Murdaugh and son won a conviction against Carl William Pauls Jr., who was charged with the murder, rape and robbery of a 73-year-old woman inside her Varnville home. The trial was held in Jasper County after a change of venue. It was heard by 14th Circuit Judge Clyde Eltzroth, Buster's former law partner. Pauls was assigned several court-appointed lawyers from Hampton and Jasper counties.

According to testimony, Pauls, 21, had signed a confession at SLED headquarters in Columbia and it was witnessed by Hampton County Sheriff Jimmy Freeman. A state psychiatrist said Pauls was emotionally disturbed and under the influence of drugs and liquor at the time of the rape, robbery and murder. The defense noted that Pauls had been abused physically and emotionally as a child, and called his mother to the stand. She wept and pleaded for mercy on her son.

Pauls was convicted, then Buster recommended that the jury sentence him to death by electrocution. The jurors deliberated for an hour and returned a sentence of life in prison for the murder, plus 25 years for the robbery.

Although the Murdaugh team generated a lot of controversy through the years, Randolph III kept his job alongside his father, and the Murdaugh family's reputation for maintaining a legal dynasty continued to grow.

In 1986, Buster Murdaugh announced that he would retire on the last day in December after serving as a prosecutor for 48 years and the 14th Circuit solicitor for all but two of them. "I'm tired," Murdaugh, 71, told the press, adding he was most proud of helping troubled young people get off the path to the penitentiary. "Putting people in the electric chair or getting them life in prison ain't no thrill at all."

Gov. Richard Riley appointed Randolph III to serve out the balance of his father's unexpired term, then he won his own election for the solicitor's job. Buster worked part-time assisting his son saying, "If y'all think you can get rid of ol' Buster — you've got another 'think' coming."

On March 20, 1987 approximately 400 people — including his fishing buddies, judges, sheriffs and the governor — threw a retirement party for him at the National Guard Armory in Hampton. Over barbecue and coleslaw, Buster, with a cigar in his mouth, grinned and listened to stories about him, and the announcement that an endowment was planned in his name to fund scholarships for students at the University of South Carolina.

In 1992 both Murdaughs were sued following the death of a Hampton County youth killed by a hit-and-run driver who had been identified but not charged. Phillip W. Mattie Jr. had been robbed, beaten and left alongside a road inside the Hampton town limits. A policeman stopped at the scene, spoke to Mattie but declined to give him a ride home. The officer suggested that the young man could hitch-hike instead. Mattie was killed by the hit-and-run driver soon afterward. The victim's father, Phillip Mattie Sr., accused the police officer of dereliction of duty and manslaughter.

But Solicitor Randolph Murdaugh III refused to indict the officer. So Mattie filed the $4.5 million lawsuit against both the solicitor and his father along with state Attorney General Travis Medlock and Hampton County Magistrate Mary F. Henderson.

The Murdaughs filed an answer and counterclaim denying most of the allegations and citing their possible legal defenses — using the Doctrine of Sovereign Immunity in the United States and the 11th Amendment to the U.S. Constitution. Both could be used to protect state and federal officials, including police officers, from legal liability in such cases.

The counterclaim accused Mattie Sr. of filing a frivolous and unfounded lawsuit as well as making false and malicious statements in local newspapers and radio broadcasts that caused the Murdaughs anxiety, emotional distress, and injury to their good names. They asked the court to dismiss the suit and require Mattie to pay the Murdaughs' legal fees as well as with actual and punitive damages. Matties' suit was dismissed.

Buster Murdaugh was 83 when he died Feb. 5, 1998 in the Hampton Regional Medical Center. He had practiced law since 1938. His obituary noted that honorary pallbearers were past and present South Carolina solicitors.

15

THE MURDAUGH WOMEN

COLUMBIA, November 1976 —

The caller was hoarse, distraught, but *The State* newspaper's obituary clerk was used to this:

"We are sorry for your loss. Please take your time ... Name of deceased?"
"Elizabeth Alexander Murdaugh," the caller said.
"Date of death and location of death?" the clerk continued ...

The State published a headlined obituary for Elizabeth A. "Libby" Murdaugh: "Civic, Church Leader Mrs. Murdaugh, Dies." The obit said Mrs. Murdaugh was the wife of 14th Circuit Assistant Solicitor Randolph Murdaugh III. The funeral and other details were being handled by the Peeples-Holland Funeral Home in Hampton.

This was before the Internet at a time when obituaries were hand-delivered or called in to newspapers by the local funeral home. It was a big story and *The State* wanted to be first to report it. But no one at the newspaper confirmed it with the funeral home. Libby was not dead. She was at home in Varnville with her husband and their four children.

Next day, *The State* published a retraction, explaining that somebody called in a hoax. "She is alive and well," the newspaper reported, adding the S.C. Law Enforcement Division and Southern Bell Telephone Company would be asked to help identify the trickster.

Gordon Rhoden was working at the Peeples-Holland Funeral Home at that time. He later became a co-owner of the home and was elected Hampton County coroner.

"This was a strange thing," Rhoden recalled. "Obviously, it did not come from our funeral home ... we don't know how or why it happened ... SLED did investigate, and we talked to them, but we still don't know why it happened or who sent it to the paper ... Of course there were rumors but I wouldn't know anything about that."

Local lawmen and the solicitor concluded the caller sought to harass, embarrass and intimidate Buster Murdaugh and his son, Randolph III. Local gossips whispered otherwise: Libby was losing her mind; she called it in herself; it was her cry for help; she sought revenge on her husband for some transgression. But there was no evidence — just rumors that made the rounds and faded away.

Family members and friends were relieved that Libby was still alive. Fact is, the men who built and maintained the Murdaugh dynasty could not have done so without their mothers and wives. The Murdaugh women were wise. They projected the family's culture and high social standing. They avoided public controversy that dogged their men, who practiced law, played politics, drank whiskey, joined hunting clubs, made front page news and appreciated an elevated status.

Stories about their wives' comings and goings peppered newspaper social pages: tea parties, bridal showers, bridge games, garden parties, flower shows, family vacations in Florida and so on. The Murdaugh women were projected as ideal wives — but certainly not the trophy variety often in the news today. "They were not accessories; they were smart, all four generations," according to Hampton historian Sam Crews. They kept the pulse of the community, were considered to be women of local high society and worked hard to keep it that way.

Annie Marvin Davis married Josiah Putman Murdaugh II. They were the parents of Randolph Murdaugh Sr., who launched the Murdaugh dynasty in 1910 when he opened his one-man law practice in Hampton County. He was elected solicitor in 1920. According to his mother's obituary, she was related to "great and illustrious statesmen," including Jefferson Davis, president of the Confederate States of America. Her obit noted that her birthplace was "the beautiful estate, Dorchester, so often mentioned by [William] Gilmore Simms," the nationally acclaimed novelist, poet and historian of Charleston.

Etta Lavinia Harvey, daughter of Hampton physician Joseph Brantley Harvey, married Randolph Murdaugh Sr. in 1914 and they had two children, Randolph "Buster" Murdaugh Jr. and John Glenn Murdaugh. She died in 1918 and Randolph Sr. married Estelle Marvin, who died in 1937. Randolph Sr. married a third woman, Mary, of which little is known. He died three years later.

Gladys Marvin married Randolph Sr.'s son "Buster" in 1937. She was a daughter of Mr. and Mrs. William Horace Marvin of Mackey Point Plantation in Jasper County. She was a graduate of Columbia College, an all-female college in South Carolina's capital city. Their wedding was at her parents' plantation house. Her obituary noted that she was well-read, a member of the Hampton-Varnville Book Club and a member of the Varnville United Methodist Church, having served as treasurer of the church's United Methodist Women for more than 40 years. She was a judge in the National Flower Show as well as a charter member and officer of the Magnolia Garden Club of Varnville.

Gladys was an elegant, intelligent woman who took great pride in her flower garden and put to good use her education in home economics (a popular major for women of that era), historian Sam Crews said, adding he and his family often worked alongside her canning home-grown fruits and vegetables. He said the Murdaugh law firm gifted her a new Cadillac each Christmas. Local stories abound about "Momma Gladys" jumping in her new Caddy and going to help friends, neighbors and others in need. Gladys died in June 1997, roughly a year before Buster passed away. Among her pallbearers were two circuit court judges.

Elizabeth "Libby" Jones Alexander Murdaugh married Randolph Murdaugh III on June 3, 1961. The Alexanders, of Brunson, were among Hampton County's founding families. Libby was an honor graduate of Columbia College, where she was a member of Alpha Kappa Gamma national leadership sorority, the Alpha Psi Omega national dramatics sorority, a three-year student government officer, and listed in *Who's Who in American Colleges and Universities.*

She helped raise three sons and a daughter in addition to teaching reading and English mostly to middle-grade students for 31 years in Hampton County School District 1. After retiring as a school teacher, she was elected to the district's board of trustees. She served multiple terms, and at one time was the chairperson.

Margaret (Maggie) Kennedy Branstetter of Summerville met Libby and Randolph III's son Alex Murdaugh at the University of South Carolina. Maggie was a member of Kappa Delta sorority and stayed in touch with many of her sisters long after she graduated from the university in 1991. She married Alex, who had played football for the Gamecocks, on Aug. 14, 1993, in Second Presbyterian Church in Charleston. He was enrolled in the USC School of Law at that time.

Maggie, like the Murdaugh women who preceded her, helped maintain the family's high social status. But unlike her mother-in-law she was not a career woman, although she briefly co-owned and operated a clothing boutique in Hampton. She enjoyed entertaining friends, who described her as spontaneous and generous. She was a "second mom" to many of her sons' friends. Maggie, Alex and sons Buster and Paul often traveled together on luxurious vacations, to Gamecocks sporting events and to the family's Edisto Beach house and the river house on Murdaugh Island.

16

The Man Called 'Handsome'

"The older I get, the more I find that temptation avoids me."
— **Randolph Murdaugh III**

HAMPTON, S.C., Sept. 20, 2018 —

Surrounded by family, friends, colleagues and admirers, Randolph Murdaugh III received the Order of the Palmetto, the state's highest civilian honor, on the lawn of the county courthouse. One by one sheriffs, lawyers, judges and others stepped to the podium and heaped praise on the man who, like his father and grandfather before him, was a lawyer and an elected solicitor.

"This is for your lifetime of service, and for what you and your family have done for the people of the Lowcountry," John E. Parker, a partner in the PMPED firm, told Murdaugh. "I am sure Buster is looking down now, so proud of Randolph."

Randolph Murdaugh III's son Alex also addressed the crowd that day. He wore a gray business suit with no tie and shared a rather odd story about his father. He recalled a night during his childhood when he and his siblings were at home with their mother waiting for his father to return.

"Daddy had been out late, 'serving the 14th Circuit'," Alex smiled and said facetiously. When his father finally arrived he told his family he was tired, got on his hands and knees, and crawled down the hallway toward the bedroom. "We thought he wanted to wrestle or something, so we all jumped on his back," Alex said, adding that his father groaned, collapsed completely and did not move. "We thought we had done killed Daddy."

Randolph III's close friends in the audience that day laughed because they knew exactly what Alex was talking about: the opening night of Hilton Head Island's new Gold Club, which featured topless women dancing in high heels, lingerie and G-strings on Aug. 10, 1991. News that a strip club was about to open had spread fast. Most folks who lived in the mostly rural five-county district were surprised. They were not used to having such establishments around, even on ritzy Hilton Head Island in Beaufort County. The island's town council and chamber of commerce had asked Beaufort Sheriff David Lucas to look into matter. The sheriff told a newspaper reporter that he had checked out the Gold Club and did not think it would violate any existing decency laws. The Associated Press picked up the story, which was published in several newspapers that covered the Lowcountry.

Solicitor Randolph Murdaugh III, who had a great sense of humor, told a reporter he would join Sheriff Lucas on the opening night of the club and monitor the situation. "For the good of the 14th Circuit, I will keep a close eye on the activities," he quipped, and that's precisely what he did. It's also why he was "knee walking" when he got home.

Randolph III, like his father, possessed not only a good sense of humor but also charisma to go along with excellent command of the law. He charmed juries with his knowledge, endeared them with his humor. His courtroom theatrics were not as dramatic or as controversial as his father's but he did have a colorful and effective style of his own. On the opening day of one trial, immediately prior to the official charges being read against two men accused of armed robbery, Randolph III called out loudly from the prosecutor's table, "Would the two defendants who committed the armed robbery please stand up!" Both suspects stood up.

Randolph III — called "Randy" in his younger days — was a skilled prosecutor and excellent personal-injury trial lawyer best known for his uncanny memory of case facts, other details and incisive interruptions of opposing counsel. During a 1989 death penalty case in Walterboro, a defense attorney making opening remarks to the jury asked rhetorically: "Did she shoot the weapon, or didn't she?" Murdaugh immediately answered loudly: "Yes!"

Randolph III enjoyed spending time with his family. While celebrating the birth of his first granddaughter, he was asked what he wanted her to call him. "Handsome," he responded, and the nickname stuck.

"Handsome" Randolph III had always wanted to follow in his father's footsteps. "From the time I was old enough to walk, I followed him around the courthouse, I wanted to be a lawyer ... I never wanted to be anything else."

Randolph III began his career as his father's assistant solicitor in 1964, and was appointed by the governor to serve the remainder of Buster Murdaugh's term upon retirement in 1986. Randolph III was elected solicitor in 1987 and stayed in office until 2005, when he retired. His father switched roles with his son and served as the assistant solicitor until he passed away.

Randolph III became a private-practice attorney in the Hampton law firm a year after his own retirement. Three generations of Randolph Murdaughs served a total 85-plus years as prosecutors in the district's solicitor's office, which is believed to be the longest period of continuous public service by members of the same family in U.S. history. Portraits of Randolph III, his father, Randolph Jr. and his grandfather, Randolph Sr., hang together on a wall inside the Hampton County Courthouse today.

Randolph III's father, Buster, sought convictions by almost any means possible and won almost all of them. But Randolph III had a different philosophy: "A prosecutor's job is not to convict but to see that justice is done," he said during a newspaper interview. "It's as much my duty to protect an innocent person as it is to prosecute a guilty person … I have never tried a person that I did not think in my mind was guilty." As solicitor, Randolph III prosecuted more than 200 murder cases and won most of them. He prided himself on his ability to know who deserved leniency, and for helping his father create the circuit's pre-trial intervention program designed to give first-time, youthful offenders a second chance.

In the *Carolina Lawyer* journal article, Randolph III was quoted as saying, "The purpose of prosecution is to end crime — that's the ultimate good. Some crimes can be stopped by a slap on the wrist; some require incarceration; some can only be stopped by electrocution."

Like the men for whom he was named, Randolph III earned numerous accolades, and throughout his long career, the Murdaugh family name remained synonymous with power and public service in the Lowcountry. And it paid off "handsomely." The Murdaughs had amassed much land and great wealth in the S.C. Lowcountry despite becoming entangled in occasional controversies. Like his father and grandfather, Randolph III was admired by constituents, peers and employees. "If you can't work for him, you can't work for anybody," said Peggy Grill, who was employed in his Hampton office for four years. "I would have worked without a paycheck. Everyone in our office respected him and the work he did in the 14th Circuit."

Like his predecessors Randolph III enjoyed the outdoors and athletics. He played football, basketball and baseball at Wade Hampton High School, and was inducted into the school's Athletics Hall of Fame. He began dating

Libby Alexander, a member of a noted Brunson family, in 1957. Libby went to Columbia College, where she was an honors student; Randolph III played football and earned a business degree at the University of South Carolina. They married in the summer of 1961 near the end of their senior years in college. Each was from prominent Hampton County families, and local newspapers reported that the wedding was lovely and well attended.

At USC, Randolph III was a member of Kappa Alpha Order, a popular social fraternity whose brothers pride themselves as "Southern gentlemen." He was vice president of his chapter and the KA representative on the inter-fraternity council. After graduation he attended the USC School of Law in Columbia and graduated in 1964. He joined the family law firm in Hampton, worked as an assistant solicitor for his father and succeeded him as the solicitor when Buster retired. Randolph III was president of the state solicitors association (1995-96) and a director on the board of the National District Attorney's Association (1998-2005).

Randolph III heard all the stories about his locally famous — at times infamous — father. He grew up in Buster Murdaugh's shadow. Portraits of his father hang in several courthouses in the 14th Judicial Circuit. His father literally and figuratively watched over him. "I never tried to fill his shoes," he said, "I've tried to do my own thing."

His father left office on Dec. 31, 1986 and Randolph III replaced him the next day. He was 47 years old at that time, and had worked for his father for 22 years when S.C. Gov. Richard Riley appointed him to fill Buster's unexpired term until being elected solicitor. Like his father, Randolph III tried cases in every county courtroom in the circuit as well as others in the state. He was a prosecutor in appeals courts and handled cases in the S.C. Supreme Court.

"You do what you've got to do, do it in a hurry and get it over with," he said. "Attention spans of jurors who don't want to be there in the first place aren't very long, and the more efficient I am in my job, the more they appreciate what I'm doing."

Randolph III handled murder, burglary, larceny, rape, child abuse, police corruption and fraud cases involving suspects who were local and from other states. In 1989 he prosecuted Mary Lynn French, 17, the daughter of a Summerville police chief, and her boyfriend, Jason Matthews, 20, of Moncks Corner, for the shooting death of Cottageville Police Chief Jerry Shelton.

French and her boyfriend were the target of a two-week search along the East Coast before their capture. Murdaugh sought the death penalty against both of them. French was found guilty of illegally possessing a pistol and sentenced to the time she had served while waiting for her trial. Matthews, 20, pleaded guilty to murdering the police chief and was sentenced to life in prison.

Also in 1989, Randolph III was the lead prosecutor in a Hampton County murder and an assistant prosecutor in a similar case in Orangeburg County. The suspect in both trials was escaped convict Dale Allen, of Sycamore, S.C. He pleaded guilty of killing his wife's ex-husband in the Orangeburg case and was found guilty of being an accessory in the shotgun slaying of his wife in Hampton. Allen, who agreed to testify against two accused accomplices, was sentenced to life in prison with the possibility of parole after 30 years.

In March 1991, Randolph III prosecuted a man known as the "Highway Killer." Michael Eugene Elkins was charged with killing, robbing and stabbing to death a Florida woman on Interstate Highway 95. Her body was found near Hardeeville, S.C., and Elkins was arrested while on the run in Dallas, where he told police, "Yeah, you got me, I did it, it's no big deal, I've been down before." Solicitor Murdaugh prosecuted him in Jasper County and won. Elkins got the death penalty, and was executed by lethal injection in 1997.

Randolph III, who shared his father's support of the death penalty, described the lengthy appeals process as a mockery of justice. In a 2018 interview published in the Hampton newspaper, he said he did not want to be remembered as a solicitor who sent killers to death row; he wanted to be known as a good prosecutor who recognized criminals that acknowledged their mistakes, were willing to turn their lives around and deserved a second chance.

However, his advocacy for mercy sometimes back-fired. Randolph III granted pre-trial leniency in 1990 for Henry Louis Wallace, accused of attempting to rape a woman in Allendale County, and released because he agreed to participate in the solicitor's office pre-trial intervention program for first-time, non-violent offenders. However, Wallace's background check failed to note his long criminal history in South Carolina and elsewhere. Murdaugh wanted to reinstate the attempted rape charge and Wallace was summoned to court, but he never showed up.

Two years later he raped a 17-year-old Rock Hill, S.C. girl at gunpoint, and two years after that he killed 11 women in North and South Carolina. By then, Wallace was known as the "Charlotte Strangler" or the "Taco Bell Strangler," depending on where the victims happened to work. He was captured, tried and convicted of killing nine of them in North Carolina. He was sent death row, where he awaits his fate.

Randolph III said Wallace was released in Hampton County because the 14th Circuit did not have easy access to national crime databases. Although Wallace's criminal history had been digitalized for databases, the solicitor's Hampton office did not have a computer in 1990.

In 1994 the solicitor got entangled in a highly publicized statewide political case. Democratic Lt. Gov. Nick Theodore was running for governor at the time and opponents accused his supporters of participating in a Democratic Party vote buying scheme, which was not unusual in South Carolina. Democratic state Rep. James Clyburn, who represented a district that included Hampton County, and other Democratic party candidates were also implicated.

Solicitor Murdaugh, a Democrat, was appointed by the governor, another Democrat, as special prosecutor to investigate the charges. Murdaugh spent a day reviewing a thick SLED file on the investigation and cleared the candidates of participating in a vote buying scheme. He said a few county election commissioners warranted further investigation, which would not be complete until after November general balloting.

The S.C. Attorney General's Office announced that it had appointed two former federal fraud investigators to review the case and wanted to present their findings to the state grand jury. Republican Party leaders accused Murdaugh of failing to be impartial while he conducted "Democrat good old boy business as usual." They noted that the PMPED law firm had donated $3,500 to Nick Theodore's campaign, and demanded that Murdaugh step down as solicitor.

Meanwhile, Theodore's opponents placed television ads saying Democrats were being investigated for paying "street money" for vote buying and fraud. "The Good Old Boys got caught again," the ads claimed. Democrats demanded that the commercials must stop.

S.C. Republican Party Chairman (later S.C. governor) Henry McMaster asked the U.S. Department of Justice to look into the matter, and for FBI Office of Public Integrity agents to fully investigate it.

"Mr. Murdaugh, after reviewing the file for a day, completely vetoes the recommendation of two independent lawyers who had been investigating for three months. It's shocking," McMaster wrote to the federal authorities. "People are going to think there is a Democrat cover-up going on."

Meanwhile, Republicans searched election records and found a document dated October 1994 by the S.C. Ethics Commission alleging that Randolph III had received a $3,200 campaign loan from his father. The money was earmarked for Randolph III's successful run to become the 14th Circuit solicitor in 1992. At that time S.C. election laws prohibited candidates from accepting campaign loans of more $1,000 from family members. A violation was a misdemeanor punishable by a $5,000 fine and up to year in jail.

McMaster renewed his call to sanction Murdaugh: "You have a man declining to investigate allegations of violations of election law, and it looks like he violated it himself." McMaster again asked the federal government to step in — a request that the U.S. District Attorney General, a Democrat, declined. Neither Murdaugh nor Theodore were prosecuted before new South Carolina election-reform efforts addressed such matters.

Randolph III retired as the 14th Circuit's full-time solicitor on Dec. 31, 2005. He joined PMPED the following year as a private-practice law partner along with his two sons, Randolph IV and Alex. Neither son ran for elected office, although Alex worked as a volunteer solicitor with Duffie Stone, Randolph III's successor. A three-generation-long Murdaugh family tradition ended when the man called "Handsome" retired.

PART TWO

17

PERFECT STORM RISING

HAMPTON, S.C., March 2019 —

Alex Murdaugh had "a tiger on his tail," a circuit court judge has said in reference to Mallory Beach's drowning. The young lady's mother, Renee, knew the Murdaugh family of lawyers had clout — a reality confirmed in February 2019 when she arrived at the bridge over Archers Creek where her daughter was missing. Authorities had not notified Renee or Mallory's father about the boating accident. Renee and her former husband heard from others that their daughter was the only passenger missing in the murky waters that morning.

Upon arrival, both parents thought it odd that officers refused to allow them to pass through to the creek. They were soon convinced behind-the-scenes finagling had begun when Maggie Murdaugh and retired solicitor Randolph Murdaugh III arrived and officers waved them through. Mallory's body was found a week later and her funeral soon followed. Renee Beach waited a month before she summoned the tiger — a scrappy, stage-four cancer survivor and attorney from Allendale who had no fear of the Murdaughs.

Lawyer Mark Tinsley lived and worked in the 14th Circuit and was a veteran of legal battles against powerful people and large corporations. He agreed to go through the courts after Alex, who owned the boat, and anyone else in politics and law enforcement who tried to help the Murdaugh family.

Tinsley filed a civil lawsuit against Alex, whose insurance company offered to settle the crash case out of court for a paltry sum. Tinsley, who regularly checked the district's court records, knew Alex had represented hundreds of clients in personal-injury cases, most of them settled in Murdaugh's favor before going to trial. Tinsley also knew Alex's youngest son, Paul, was a heavy drinker with a fiery temper fueled by alcohol.

Alex was furious about the Beaches' lawsuit. The six-foot-four former USC football player known as Big Red spotted Mark Tinsley at a cocktail party at a lawyers' conference on Hilton Head Island. He stormed through the crowd and confronted his Allendale adversary: "Hey, Bo, what's this I've been hearing about what you've been saying? I thought we were friends."

Tinsley didn't hesitate: "Alex, we are friends, but if you don't think I can burn your house down … you're wrong. You need to settle this case."

Alex was in no mood to cooperate, especially during the discovery process regarding his finances. Month after month passed, so Tinsley filed a motion accusing Murdaugh of ignoring his requests for information. He asked the court to compel complete disclosure of Alex's financial records. Finally, two years after the accident, a showdown hearing was scheduled for June 10, 2021 before Judge Daniel Hall. As it turned out, June 10, 2021, was three days after the murders of Maggie and Paul Murdaugh.

In the meantime word got around the PMPED office that Alex had restructured payments for his share of year-end legal fees collected by the firm. When PMPED's managing partner Ronnie Crosby heard about Alex's new pay plan, he told the firm's chief financial officer Jeannie Seckinger:

"Oh f--- no, he's not (going to restructure his pay). Keep an eye on Alex, learn as much as you can about it, and keep me informed." (Crosby later testified, "We absolutely were not going to participate in anything illegal or unethical that would subject us to liability or create issues with the South Carolina Bar.")

While Seckinger monitored Alex's money moves and news about the boat crash spread, Maggie Murdaugh stayed more and more at the house at Edisto Beach. Things seemed to be spinning out of control in Hampton: the Beach lawsuit against Alex loomed large and the media's barrage of coverage about Paul and the boat crash intensified. Maggie thought people in Hampton were snubbing her, and she feared her husband was abusing opioids again. She asked Paul, her "little detective," to find out what his father was up to.

Alex was in Hampton on May 26, 2021 when he got a text from Paul, who was with his mother at the beach house: "I'm still in Edisto Beach because when you get here, we have to talk. Mom found several bags of pills in your computer bag."

Maggie had also done some detective work on her own: she typed "white pill 30 on one side rp" on her computer's search bar, and moments later up popped "Oxycodone Hydrochloride. 30 milligrams" on the screen. Maggie knew Alex had long taken prescribed drugs to ease the pain of his recurring football injuries. She remembered the night he mixed pain medicine with too much alcohol and became extremely aggressive, practically incoherent. Alex drove Maggie to his parents' house in Almeda and did not apologize for his behavior until the next day. But that was then and this is now, she thought as she read her computer screen.

After Paul told Alex that Maggie found his bag of pills, he texted his wife: "I am very sorry that I do this to all of you. I love you." Alex was addicted to opiates and did not want to endure the misery of detoxification. He also knew a lot of money could be made selling the little white pills at the center of his life. He drove to Edisto Beach, was confronted by Maggie and promised to clean up his act.

Almost two weeks later, on June 7, Alex was late getting to work. This was not unusual, and neither was his habit of working frantically throughout the day and into the evening hours. The paralegals joked about his erratic work routine and odd personality. One of them described Alex as a Tasmanian devil — red-headed, loud, hyperactive and unpredictable.

Alex's work ethic and depth of knowledge about the law had long been questionable. Still he excelled in his ability to read people, intimidate opponents, manipulate his clients, convince them that jurors would rule in his favor if need be, and their cases would be settled out of court. It was in his blood. Alex knew the "art of bullshit," the law firm's CFO Seckinger later testified.

Alex did make a lot of money, but never enough to satisfy his needs. The firm paid each partner an annual salary of $125,000 — chump change compared to what the firm collected from personal-injury cases, most of them settled before going to trial. The partners got hefty year-end bonuses based on the firm's generous performance-based profit-sharing program. Since his great-grandfather, grandfather and father were, in effect, the principal owners and operators of the firm, Alex had little trouble bending the rules about the way he received his year-end payments. If questioned internally, Alex would offer an excuse and pay back at least some of what he owed.

But that changed after Alex's paralegal Annette Griswold told CFO Seckinger that a $792,000 check to PMPED from the Wilson Law Firm in Bamberg was missing. Chris Wilson and Alex were close friends who had shared civil cases. Chris asked Alex to help prosecute the personal-injury case in question, and it was settled in their favor. Chris was paid the full amount for services rendered and sent Alex's law firm two checks, one to cover PMPED's expenses and the other for $792,000 — half of what Alex said he was owed for the getting the settlement. Seckinger had heard that Alex had been sued by Mallory's mother, and suspected he might try to hide his payment, which was supposed to be processed through the firm as per PMPED policy. Where was Chris Wilson's check?

Alex was tall, wide framed, and filled the hallway outside his office as he combed through records in his file cabinet. "What you need now?" he snapped when Seckinger approached. Alex was rather odd — everyone in the office knew it — but never before had he been so obviously rude. He wasn't raised that way.

Stunned, Seckinger asked about Wilson's missing check, saying $792,000 was a lot of money. Alex told her to join him in the privacy of his office. Once inside, she said, "I have reason to believe you received those fees yourself, and I need proof that you did not."

Alex offered a ready answer: the money was still in Chris Wilson's trust account because Alex's friend wasn't sure about the best way to structure the settlement payout. That's when, as usual, Alex's cellphone rang. He was known around the office for his annoying cell-phone habits, which included interrupting meetings to answer calls. Alex would take a call while having sex, his colleagues joked among themselves. So it was no surprise when he cut off Seckinger and answered his phone. Alex no longer sounded angry, she remembered, as he responded to the caller.

"What's wrong?" Seckinger asked.

"It's Handsome. He's dying."

Seckinger knew who he was talking about. Everyone in the firm loved Alex's father.

It was early June 2021 and Alex Murdaugh had many reasons to be distraught:

— He faced a multimillion-dollar-lawsuit because he owned the boat from which Mallory Beach was thrown and died.

— His son Paul, who was drunk and drove the boat the night it crashed in Archers Creek, faced a criminal trial.

— His wife, Maggie, found his bag of opioids.

— The chief financial officer of his law firm confronted him about his hidden assets and missing fees.

— His father, Alex's protector and source of cash when he needed it, was dying.

Alex Murdaugh was at the center of a perfect storm threatening to destroy his privileged life, and that of his family.

18

MAYHEM AT MOSELLE

ISLANDTON, S.C., June 7, 2021 —

It was dusk when dark clouds crept over Moselle, the Murdaughs' hunting estate straddling the river that separates Colleton and Hampton counties. Heat lightning illuminated distant skies. The temperature almost matched the 89 percent humidity outside. It was a typical summer evening in the Lowcountry when merely the thought of leaving an air-conditioned house makes you sweat.

Despite the miserable mugginess, Paul Murdaugh, 22, and his mother, Maggie, 52, were at the kennels, several hundred yards away from the main house, checking on a hunting dog named Cash, whose owner was a family friend who had boarded the chocolate-color retriever at Moselle. The sun was setting. The family's guinea hens and chickens began roosting on dust-covered farm vehicles and other equipment under an adjacent shed. Caged hounds barked steadily hoping to get fed or, even better, released for a night of hunting raccoons. Paul was wrapping up a cellphone video and conversation with Cash's owner about an injury on the dog's tail when the voices of Maggie and a man who sounded like Alex were recorded.

Moments later, Paul's executioner, who had two loaded weapons — a semi-automatic, AR-style rifle and a 12-gauge Benelli Super Black Eagle shotgun — at his disposal, started shooting. Paul was standing just inside the door when the killer shouldered the shotgun, stepped in front of the door and pulled the trigger. The blast was deafening. Buckshot ripped through Paul's left breast and arm at 1,200 feet per second, spun him around almost face to face with his executioner. Gunpowder seared Paul's torso; the muzzle was so close that the shell's plastic wadding between the powder and the shot embedded below the young man's armpit. His blood splattered the wall behind him.

The killer had planned to put the shotgun down, deftly grab the rifle, which he had leaned on a wall left of the feed room door, and kill Maggie:

two bodies, two guns, one shooter. Surely investigators would assume more than one killer was involved. But Paul stayed on his feet. The buckshot had ripped through the young man's fat tissue and muscle but missed vital organs. Hunched over, his arm and head dripping blood, Paul lurched toward the gunman, who did not have time to shoulder the shotgun again. He held it low and slightly upward to Paul's face and fired again.

More than a hundred smaller pellets grazed the top of Paul's shoulder, entered his neck near the base of his skull and ripped away his brain stem. Gases from the blast exploded the right side of his cranium and took most of his brain with it. Paul fell face first through the door, across a concrete walkway toward the yard. His body sprawled across the walkway, his feet just inside the feed room.

Maggie apparently was headed toward the house when she heard the first shotgun blast. She turned around and ran to the kennels, close enough to witness the second blast. The killer dropped the shotgun, grabbed the rifle and fired in quick succession two .300-caliber Blackout rounds into Maggie's gut. They pierced the abdominal wall and tore through her intestines, pancreas and left kidney. Maggie doubled over and fell to her hands and knees. The killer circled behind her as she tried to crawl toward her son and fired again. The round entered Maggie's torso, ripped through her left breast and the left side of her face before striking in her brain. She was dead when the killer fired another round at close range into the back of her head near the base of her skull.

It was like a scene in a film based on a theme from an ancient Greek tragedy: bloody bodies of a prominent mother and her son, hapless victims of a heartless executioner; caged hounds baying in the aftermath; lightning and thunder and tears from dark clouds over Moselle starting to fall.

Later in media interviews with people who knew him well, Paul was described as a loyal friend who loved to fish and hunt in the woods and fields, swamps and rivers of the Lowcountry. He was energetic, often mischievous, a child of privilege who preferred playing outside in dirt over waiting for his mother to light birthday candles so he could make a wish. In high school his closest friends had noticed Paul could not hold his liquor. His personality changed dramatically. It was as if he had become another person — angry, argumentative, ready to fight — a tortured young man that his friends nicknamed "Timmy."

Maggie Murdaugh seemed to enjoy life. She had raised two popular sons, and her family lived in two beautiful houses. She did not have to work outside home because she did not have to support her family financially. She drove new cars. She had many friends. She looked forward to reunions with her sorority sisters at the University of South Carolina, and enjoyed going with Alex and the boys to watch the Gamecocks play football, baseball and basketball. She often entertained guests at the beach house, took spontaneous shopping trips to Savannah and Charleston.

"Maggie had a heart of pure generosity and loved welcoming friends and family into her home on any given occasion," her obituary said. "She adored her family and cherished spending time on the boat with her two sons. She will be remembered as a 'second mom' to her sons' many friends ..."

But not everyone loved Maggie, and the word on Hampton streets was not always kind: "Her nose was stuck so far up in the air that when it rained she might drown," and after she died, "What happened to her is karma."

On the night of June 7, Alex Murdaugh returned to Moselle after a quick trip to see his mother in Almeda, about 13 miles away. At 10:07 p.m. he dialed 911 and a Hampton County dispatcher answered. The call was quickly transferred to a dispatcher in Colleton County:

Alex: *This is Alex Murdaugh at 4147 Moselle Road. I need the police and an ambulance immediately. My wife and child have been shot badly ... I've been up to it now, it's bad!*

Dispatcher: *OK, are they breathing?*

Alex: *No ma'am.*

Dispatcher: *You said it's your wife and your son?*

Alex: *My wife and my son.*

Dispatcher: *Are they in a vehicle?*

Alex: *No ma'am. They're on the ground out at my kennel.* (His voice is garbled. He sounds out of breath, incoherent at times.)

Dispatcher: *OK, and did you see anyone?* (The response is garbled.) *OK, is he* (the son) *breathing at all?*

Alex: *No. Nobody is!*

Again, the dispatcher asked if the victims were breathing. Gasping between what sounds like sobs, Alex said he had checked each pulse and found none. The dispatcher asked if they had shot themselves. "Oh, hell no," he responded, then mentioned that his son had been involved in a fatal boating accident in Beaufort, and had been receiving threats ever since.

A code-three alert was issued for Colleton County. Emergency responders and sheriff's deputies turned on their lights and sirens and drove to Moselle. Upon arrival, they saw near the kennels Alex Murdaugh and the bodies, both face down and covered in blood. Dogs barked incessantly; stench of kennels and human carnage permeated the air. Spent rifle casings were on the ground at a corner of the shed; two empty shotgun shells were on the kennel's concrete walkway near Paul's body. State Law Enforcement Division investigators were summoned; a special crime-scene unit was dispatched from Columbia.

It had been raining at Moselle, and a pink sheet was placed over Paul's body and a pop-up canopy was erected over Maggie's remains. Alex — wearing clean olive-green shorts, a white T-shirt and running shoes — stood nearby when the state agents got there.

Prior to that, Colleton Sheriff's Detective Laura Rutland, one of the first officers to arrive at Moselle, asked Alex what had happened. He told her he had visited his ailing mother at her house in Almeda, returned home and soon found the bodies of his wife and son. He said he checked both Maggie and Paul for vital signs, then mentioned that Paul had received numerous threats since the fatal boat crash in Beaufort. He told the detective he was certain the deaths of his son and wife were not a murder/suicide. He again referenced the boat crash then suggested the killings might be a result of backwoods justice, and named possible suspects.

Detective Rutland checked the kennel area and noticed blood and brain matter mixed with water around Paul's body. She thought it was odd there were no bloody knee or foot prints on the concrete, as she noted Alex had said he checked the bodies for vital signs. She also noted Alex's hands, arms, clothes and shoes were clean, and that, when she had interviewed Alex, his shirt smelled freshly laundered.

The SLED crime team arrived at Moselle at 12:07 a.m. on June 8, and assumed control of the crime scene. Later that morning Alex got into the front passenger seat of a SLED vehicle next to SLED Senior Special Agent

David Owen, who was behind the wheel. Detective Laura Rutland, who was Colleton County's liaison to SLED, was seated behind Murdaugh and next to Danny Henderson, a lawyer and one of Alex's best friends. The agents recorded the interview, while Alex did most of the talking — sometimes emotionally, sometimes not. He repeated much of what he earlier told Detective Rutland. He was very specific about when and where he last saw Maggie and Paul alive.

The Murdaugh murders made the national news, and questions quickly multiplied. Who killed Maggie and Paul? Was it retribution for Mallory Beach's death two years prior, and what exactly was Paul's role in the boating accident? Where was Alex when the shooting started?

The day after the murders, the Beach family authorized a message to the public:

"The Beach family extends its deepest and warmest sympathies to the Murdaughs during this terrible time. Having suffered the devastating loss of their own daughter, the family prays that the Murdaughs can find some level of peace from this tragic loss. They would like the family and the community to know that their thoughts and continued prayers are with the Murdaughs. It is their most sincere hope that someone will come forward and cooperate with authorities so that the perpetrator of these senseless crimes can be brought to justice."

The same day, local and state police issued an odd statement about the murders: "At this time, there is no danger to the public." It mentioned no suspects, and asked anyone with information about the killings to call a certain number.

On June 10, the day before both Maggie's and Paul's funerals, Alex's father, Randolph Murdaugh III, 81, died after a long bout with cancer. Also that day Alex gave a second statement to state agents while sitting in a cruiser at his brother John Marvin Murdaugh's hunting lodge near Almeda. Investigators told Alex that they needed to talk again before removing him from a "circle" of others at the center of their investigation. Alex proceeded to tell SLED Special Agent Jeff Croft and the others about a pleasant ride he and Paul had taken around the Moselle property on the afternoon of the evening Maggie and Paul were murdered.

That's as far as Alex got before he choked up and cried. The agents comforted Alex, handed him tissues. He composed himself and continued, saying the last time he saw Maggie and Paul alive was during an early supper inside the Moselle house. He said he took a nap then left in his truck for his parents' house at Almeda to check on his mother. He said his father had been fighting cancer and was in the hospital.

When asked about his relationship with Maggie, Alex said, "I had a wonderful wife, she was a great mother. She didn't work but she took care of me and the boys." At the conclusion of the interview, an agent downloaded data from Alex's cellphone. Alex was asked to spit out a wad of tobacco he was chewing and take an oral buccal swab for a DNA sample. Alex then said what sounded like: "It's just so bad … I did him so bad!" Later, after agents listened carefully to the recording, they were not sure what they heard. Did Alex say, "They (not 'I') did him so bad?" The recording was not clear.

In less than a week, members of the Murdaugh family attended three funerals of their own: Maggie, Paul and Randolph III. On June 16, *The Hampton County Guardian* learned that divers were searching the Big Salkehatchie River roughly two miles from the crime scene. The newspaper also heard that SLED dive teams were searching ponds and swampland on the Moselle property for the murder weapons and other evidence.

On June 17, after more than a week with no arrests and no announced leads in the case, Alex's brothers, Randy and John Marvin, were on ABC's "Good Morning America" show pleading for help in finding the killers and saying Paul had earlier received death threats. "The persons who did this are out there," Randy said. "We need help finding who did this … We're just regular people, and we are hurting just like (the viewers) would be hurting if it had happened to them."

The plot thickened on June 23 when state authorities released the following statement: "SLED has opened an investigation into the death of Stephen Smith, 19, based upon information gathered during the course of the double-murder investigation of Paul and Maggie Murdaugh." It had long been rumored that Smith, a homosexual, had a relationship with Paul's brother, Buster, while all three were in high school. Smith's body was found in 2015 on a paved rural road in Hampton County not far from Moselle. Authorities had ruled he died when hit by a truck whose unknown driver had left the scene of the accident.

On June 25, Alex and his surviving son, Buster, offered a $100,000 reward for information leading to the arrest and conviction of anyone responsible for the murders of Maggie and Paul. "I want to thank everyone for the incredible love and support that we have received over the last few weeks," Alex said in the statement. "Now is the time to bring justice for Maggie and Paul ..." He also said a deadline for the information was Sept. 30, 2021 — approximately three months away — which seemed rather odd. Was Alex trying to divert attention away from the renewal of an investigation of Stephen Smith's death six years ago?

SLED released little information about anything throughout its investigation, and the few reports it did offer were vague and heavily redacted. The Charleston-based *Post and Courier* newspaper filed a Freedom of Information Act complaint against SLED and the Colleton County Sheriff's Office accusing the agencies of withholding information, including Alex's 911 tapes, about the murders.

On July 22, almost 45 days after the murders, SLED released Alex Murdaugh's chilling 911 call, which was widely reported and analyzed in the media. Was Alex telling the truth? Did he arrive back at Moselle, find the bodies of his loved ones and call 911, or was he there when they died? Did he participate in the murders of his wife and son?

As days turned to months, the absence of facts sparked speculation and several conspiracy theories. One especially odd rumor circulated on social media: vehicles were found buried on the 1,700-acre Moselle property including one that was used in the 2015 death of Stephen Smith. Soon SLED released another statement: "The rumor referencing vehicles being unearthed on property owned by the Murdaughs is unfounded. SLED has inquired with Lowcountry law enforcement and found no credibility to the rumors currently circulating online."

This increased interest on social media about the Murdaugh murders. Chat rooms were packed with speculators; podcasts devoted solely to the case popped up everywhere. The Murdaughs' current lives, their family's history and numerous unconfirmed details about the murders were broadcast on radio, television and digital media. Most theories were believable: Maggie was about to leave Alex. He shot his wife with the rifle, then took the shotgun from Paul and killed his son. Alex hired hitmen to kill Maggie and Paul.

The Murdaugh saga was featured on CBS television's "48 Hours," ABC

"20/20" and "Dateline NBC." Family photographs of Alex, Maggie and their children were in newspapers, magazines, newscasts, tabloids and blogs. The Murdaugh murders made news in the U.S, in Great Britain and elsewhere in Europe. Netflix and HBO Max documentary crews scoured the Lowcountry, interviewing people who knew the family and filming key sites. Motion picture executives from California came calling. The double-murder mystery intrigued millions from all over. It was a nightmare for most folks in Hampton County.

"They are not the monsters the media outlets are portraying them to be," Tangie Peeples Ohmer, a Murdaugh family friend, told *The Hampton County Guardian*. "My problem with all of this is that, regardless of how anyone feels about Paul's past, a family lost a son, a grandson, a brother, nephew and cousin ... and Maggie paid the ultimate price as well." Another local, Katlyn Ginn, agreed: "A family just had their world turned upside down ... (they) have my prayers, and love is being sent their way as they have a very tough journey ahead."

On Aug. 11, Alex met again with SLED agents. He was accompanied this time by his close friend and attorney Cory Fleming of Beaufort for what they thought would be an update on the case. But SLED agent David Owen asked Alex about two missing family weapons: a Benelli shotgun and an AR rifle that fired 300 Blackout rounds. Owen said DNA found at the murder scene belonged to Alex, and that a Snapchat video posted by Paul on the afternoon of his death showed his father wearing an outfit different than what he wore when the police arrived that night at Moselle. Also, according to SLED's taped interview with Alex:

Owen: *"I just have two more questions ...* "Did you kill Maggie?" Alex was stunned. It was the first time any investigator had directly challenged him.
Alex: *"No!"*
Owen: *"Do you know who did?"*
Alex: *"No, I do not know who did it."*
Owen: *"Did you kill Paul?"*
Alex: *"No, sir. I did not kill Paul."*
Owen: *"Do you know who did?"*
Alex: *"No, sir, I do not know who did ... Do you think I killed Maggie?"*
Owen: *"I have to go where the evidence and the facts take me."*

Alex: *"I understand that ... Do you think I killed Paul?"*

Owen: *"I have to go where the evidence and the facts take me, and I don't have anything that points to anyone else at this time."*

Alex: *"So, does that mean I am a suspect?"*

Owen: *"You are still in this ... I have to set my beliefs aside and go with the facts."*

SLED agents had asked the FBI for help, and Owen got top investigators who had advanced technology at his disposal. But two key pieces of evidence posed problems. They had Paul's cellphone but did not know the password, and they needed access to GPS data captured in Alex's GM vehicle, which he had driven from Moselle to his parents' house and back the evening of the murders. In addition, SLED investigators had yet to find the murder weapons. All they had was circumstantial evidence.

Meanwhile, 14th Circuit Solicitor Duffie Stone asked to recuse himself from involvement in the murders as he had done with the fatal boat crash two years prior. In an Aug. 11 letter to S.C. Attorney General Alan Wilson, Stone wrote:

"Considering the events of today in SLED's investigation of the homicides of Paul and Maggie Murdaugh, I am asking that you assume all prosecutorial functions in this matter effective immediately. By copy of this letter, I am informing (SLED) Chief Mark Keel of my decision to recuse myself from prosecuting these cases."

Meanwhile, SLED had a suspect but did not have any earth-shattering evidence, no murder weapons and no eyewitnesses.

19

CHICKENS HOME TO ROOST

HAMPTON, S.C., Sept. 4, 2021 —

On a sunny Saturday on Labor Day weekend Alex Murdaugh stood beside his dead wife's black Mercedes SUV on the side of Old Salkehatchie Road, heart racing and head bleeding from a gunshot wound. His wife and youngest son were murdered almost three months earlier. Now he was a suspect in the killings and investigators were nipping ever closer at his heels. On Friday his law partners had called Alex in for a come-to-Jesus meeting, accused him of stealing hundreds of thousands of dollars from the firm and refused to let him slide this time. Excuses about mistakenly cashing checks and charging extravagant expenses to the company credit card were no longer acceptable. And his father, Randolph "Handsome" Murdaugh III, was dead, and could no longer bail out his son.

The firm's Labor Day statement, issued soon after Alex met Friday with the partners, was damning:

"On Friday, Sept. 3, 2021, Alex Murdaugh resigned from the Law Firm. He is no longer associated with PMPED in any manner. His resignation came after the discovery by PMPED that Alex misappropriated funds in violation of PMPED standards and policies. A forensic accounting firm will be retained to conduct a thorough investigation. Law enforcement and the S.C. Bar have been notified by PMPED. This is disappointing news for all of us. Rest assured that our firm will deal with this in a straightforward manner. There's no place in our firm for such behavior… "

"The truth always comes back and bites you in the ass," is a local expression applied to situations like this. In South Carolina, if a lady is within earshot, the adage is presented more politely: "The chickens always come home to roost." For the first time in Alex's life of extreme privilege and limited talent, the former Gamecock football player nicknamed "Big Red" was in very serious trouble. His dad was dead, and family friends in law enforcement and his partners in law had him by his tailfeathers. The once impenetrable walls of the family coop were breeched and the roof was falling in on Alex. At 1:34 p.m. on the Saturday of Labor Day weekend, Alex Murdaugh was alone, bleeding from the back of his head, standing next to his late wife's luxury SUV on a little-used country road not far from his parents' house in Almeda. He lifted his cellphone and dialed 911:

Alex: *I got a flat tire and I stopped, and somebody stopped to help me and when I turned my back, they tried to shoot me.*
Dispatcher: *Oh, OK. Were you shot?*
Alex: *Yes, but I mean I'm OK.*
Dispatcher: *You ... shot where? Where were you shot at?*
Alex: *Huh?*
Dispatcher: *Did they actually shoot you or try to shoot you?*
Alex: *They shot me.*
Dispatcher: *OK. You need EMS?*
Alex: *Well, I mean, yes, I can't drive ... I'm bleeding, a lot.*

Also at that time a passing driver called 911 and said she saw an injured man standing beside a black Mercedes on the side of Old Salkehatchie Road and waving his hands for help. The passerby, who did not stop, said the man had red hair and might be bleeding. "It kind of looks like a setup," the caller told the dispatcher.

Hampton County sheriff's deputies soon arrived at the scene, then called for a medevac helicopter to take Alex to a Savannah hospital. Later, a medical report noted that his scalp was lacerated, had a small, subdural hemorrhage (near his brain and upper spine) as well as a slight skull fracture. Alex had also tested positive for having barbiturates and opiates in his system. All of which triggered a new line of intrigue on social media, television and radio as well as in hundreds of newspapers. Who shot Alex Murdaugh, and why? Was it connected to the murders of his wife and son? Were other members of the Murdaugh family at risk?

The chickens had indeed come home to roost, and the House of Murdaugh was seriously shaking, about to fall.

Alex Murdaugh's boat wrecked and aground in Archers Creek. The deadly 2019 boat crash launched lawsuits and criminal investigations that led to the fall of the House of Murdaugh. Photo courtesy of the S.C Attorney General's Office.

Lowcountry mud and blood on the deck of the Murdaugh family boat after the February 2019 boat crash that claimed the life of Mallory Beach and injured several others. Photo courtesy of the S.C. Attorney General's Office.

Nineteen-year-old Mallory Beach with one of her pets. She was an animal lover and college student from Hampton County who died in the 2019 boating accident. Photo courtesy of *The Hampton County Guardian.*

Cooler of alcoholic beverages found following the boat crash that took the life of Mallory Beach in Beaufort County waters. Photo courtesy of the S.C. Attorney General's Office.

The official logo for the Mal's Palz nonprofit foundation. Photo courtesy of *The Hampton County Guardian.*

Former 14th Circuit Solicitor and PMPED founder Randolph Murdaugh Sr. in front of his Varnville home, circa 1920-1940. Photo courtesy of *The Hampton County Guardian* archives.

Beaufort County police booking photograph of Paul Terry Murdaugh. It was taken in his street clothes. He never went to jail. Photo courtesy of the S.C. Attorney General's Office.

The PMPED law firm's office in Hampton is one of the tallest buildings in rural Hampton County. Photo by Michael M. DeWitt Jr.

This portrait of Randolph "Buster" Murdaugh Jr. adorns a wall of the Hampton County Courthouse, along with portraits of his father and son. Photo courtesy of *The Hampton County Guardian.*

A young Richard Alexander "Alex" Murdaugh on the pages of a Wade Hampton High School yearbook. Photo courtesy of *The Hampton County Guardian.*

Paul Murdaugh at his arraignment and bond hearing in a Beaufort County courtroom on charges of felony boating under the influence of alcohol resulting in death. Photo courtesy of *The Hampton County Guardian.*

Randolph Murdaugh III (left) and his father, Buster, confer outside the Jasper County Courthouse during a murder trial. Newspaper clipping courtesy of *The Hampton County Guardian*.

A wooden cross marks the spot where Stephen Smith's body was found on Sandy Run Road in Hampton County. Photo by Michael M. DeWitt Jr.

In this Wade Hampton High School yearbook photo, Alex Murdaugh is at right on the sidelines as a Red Devil football player. Murdaugh was once named Most Athletic and played multiple sports. Photo courtesy of *The Hampton County Guardian*.

Near the end of his career, Buster Murdaugh speaks at a legal convention on Hilton Head Island. Photo courtesy of *The Hampton County Guardian*.

Randolph Murdaugh III poses in his Hampton office in 2018, the year he was awarded the Order of the Palmetto, South Carolina's highest civilian honor. Photo by Michael M. DeWitt Jr.

Randolph Murdaugh III makes a speech from the second-floor balcony of the Hampton County Courthouse. Photo by Michael M. DeWitt Jr.

The Hampton County Detention Center's booking photograph of Alex Murdaugh. Photo courtesy of the Hampton County Sheriff's Office.

Margaret "Maggie" Murdaugh and her youngest son, Paul Terry Murdaugh. Photo courtesy of *The Hampton County Guardian.*

One entrance to Moselle, the vast Murdaugh estate straddling Hampton and Colleton counties where Maggie and Paul Murdaugh were slain. Photo by Michael M. DeWitt Jr.

South Carolina Attorney General Alan Wilson led the overall investigation and prosecution of Alex Murdaugh. Photo courtesy of the S.C. Attorney General's Office.

Allendale attorney Mark Tinsley argues his case during a pre-trial hearing in the wrongful-death suit filed by the estate of Mallory Beach. Photo by Michael M. DeWitt Jr.

This portrait of a young Gloria Satterfield was on display during the public announcement of the Gloria's Gift Foundation in 2022. Photo by Robert Daley/Chatham Photo.

Grieving but proud, Sandy Smith stands behind a memorial erected for her late son, Stephen, in Hampton County during the summer of 2022. Photo courtesy of *The Hampton County Guardian*.

The family of the late Gloria Satterfield pose with their attorneys during the announcement of Gloria's Gift. Photo by Robert Daley/Chatham Photo.

The Colleton County Courthouse in Walterboro.

Murdaugh enters the Colleton County courtroom for the first of several pre-trial hearings on his double murder charges. Photo by Michael M. DeWitt Jr.

Murdaugh is sworn in during a pretrial hearing in Colleton County in 2022. Photo by Michael M. DeWitt Jr.

From left are Murdaugh defense attorneys Jim Griffin and Richard Harpootlian. At right is Creighton Waters, the state's lead prosecutor in the Murdaugh murder case. Photo by Michael M. DeWitt Jr.

Prosecutor Creighton Waters (left) asks witness Jeff Croft, a SLED senior special agent, questions about weapons and ammunition collected from Alex Murdaugh's Moselle property during the double-murder trial at the Colleton County Courthouse. Photo by Joshua Boucher/*The State*/pool.

Colleton County Sheriff Sgt. Daniel Greene testifies in the Alex Murdaugh murder trial at the Colleton County Courthouse in Walterboro. Photo by Grace Beahm Alford of *The Post and Courier.*

Assistant prosecutor David Fernandez (left) and Murdaugh family friend Nathan Tuten look at a rifle found at Moselle during the double-murder trial in Walterboro. Photo by Andrew J. Whitaker of *The Post and Courier*.

Jeanne Seckinger, law firm chief financial officer, testifies during the murder trial about missing money from her Hampton County office. Photo by Joshua Boucher/*The State*/ Pool.

Hampton lawyer Ronnie Crosby testifies during the murder trial of his former law partner Alex Murdaugh. Photo by Andrew J. Whitaker of *The Post and Courier.*

Prosecutor John Meadors shows a photo of a raincoat to witness Mushelle "Shelly" Smith, caregiver for Alex's mother, Libby Murdaugh, in February 2023, during the double murder trial of Alex Murdaugh at the Colleton County Courthouse. Photo by Jeff Blake/*The State*/Pool.

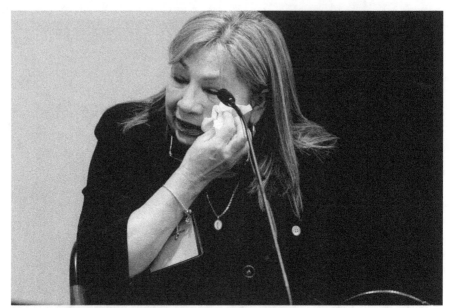

Blanca Turrubiate-Simpson answers questions from prosecutor John Meadors during Alex Murdaugh's trial for murder at the Colleton County Courthouse. Photo by Joshua Boucher/*The State*/Pool.

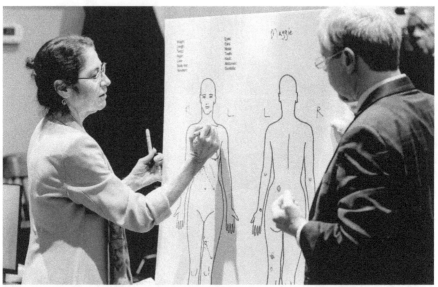

Forensic pathologist at MUSC Dr. Ellen Riemer describes the gun wounds to Maggie Murdaugh's body as prosecutor Creighton Waters looks on during day 16 of the double murder trial of Alex Murdaugh at the Colleton County Courthouse. The black marks indicate entrance wounds; the red marks indicate exit wounds. Photo by Jeff Blake/*The State*/Pool.

Prosecutor John Meadors questions SLED agent David Owen during Alex Murdaugh's murder trial at the Colleton County Courthouse in Walterboro. Photo by Grace Beahm Alford of *The Post and Courier.*

Crime-scene specialist Kenneth Kinsey shows how cartridges might have been ejected from the shotgun used to kill Paul Murdaugh during Alex Murdaugh's murder trial. Photo by Joshua Boucher/*The State*/Pool.

Left to right, John Marvin Murdaugh, Buster Murdaugh, Buster's girlfriend Brooklynn White and Lynn Murdaugh Goette listen to testimony during the trial of Alex Murdaugh at the Colleton County Courthouse. Photo by Andrew J. Whitaker of *The Post and Courier*.

Alex Murdaugh gives tearful testimony during his double-murder trial. Photo by Grace Beahm Alford of *The Post and Courier*.

Alex "Buster" Murdaugh Jr. (second from right) looks over to his father after Judge Clifton Newman charged the jury during the murder trial in Walterboro. Photo by Joshua Boucher/*The State*/Pool.

Defense attorney Dick Harpootlian holds a 300 Blackout rifle similar to the one used to kill Maggie Murdaugh. Mike Sutton, a forensic engineer for the defense, looks on during day 21 of the double-murder trial. Photo by Jeff Blake/*The State*/ Pool.

Judge Clifton Newman places down his gavel after sentencing Alex Murdaugh to life in prison for killing his wife Maggie and son Paul at the family hunting retreat known as Moselle. Photo by Andrew J. Whitaker of *The Post and Courier.*

Alex Murdaugh is helped from the stand by his attorney Dick Harpootlian after being found guilty on all four charges: two counts of murder and two counts of possessing a weapon during a violent crime. Photo by Andrew J. Whitaker of *The Post and Courier*.

Murdaugh and a Colleton County court officer following the sentencing phase of the double-murder trial. Murdaugh was sentenced to life in prison. Photo by Andrew J. Whitaker of *The Post and Courier*.

S.C. Attorney General Alan Wilson gives a congratulatory hug to Prosecutor Creighton Waters after Alex Murdaugh was found guilty of killing his wife and son. Photo by Andrew J. Whitaker of *The Post and Courier.*

Soon after the conclusion of the murder trial, flowers and memorials were placed by family, friends and others on the graves of Maggie and Paul Murdaugh in the Hampton Cemetery. Photo by Michael M. DeWitt Jr.

20

THE UNRAVELING

More than two years had passed since the cold February morning when Mallory Beach died after being thrown from Alex Murdaugh's boat into tidal water under the Archers Creek bridge near Beaufort. Maggie and Paul were murdered in June 2021 and three months later on Sept. 4, somebody shot Alex in the head as he stood beside his car on Old Salkehatchie Road. He was airlifted to a Savannah hospital where it was determined his head wound was minor but his bloodstream was polluted with opiates and other drugs.

Alex first told police he was shot by a young, clean-cut stranger. Authorities soon determined it was Alex's scruffy associate Curtis Smith, 61. His truck was captured on a nearby church's security camera following Alex's black Mercedes on Old Salkehatchie Road. It was an obvious set-up.

Meanwhile, story after story about the bizarre life and times of Alex Murdaugh and family entertained the general public in what read like a serialized crime novel in newspapers across the nation and beyond. Millions of people — most of whom had never set foot in the lowlands of Hampton County, S.C. — followed the unfolding drama. As each new twist was reported, the noose tightened around Big Red's neck.

Alex Murdaugh and his high-powered defense team initially told police he was driving his late wife's car on Old Salkehatchie Road when a dash light indicated a tire was losing air. They said Alex stopped the car, got out and was checking the tire when a man in a pickup truck arrived and asked if he needed help. Murdaugh was responding when the stranger raised a pistol, shot Alex and fled. But the story was full of holes, and savvy journalists knew it. Alex's head wound was superficial, barely noticeable in news clips of him leaving the hospital. They noted this and included Alex's previous condition: he was a prime suspect in the murders of his wife and youngest son, and his law partners accused him of stealing money from clients as well as themselves before kicking him out of the prestigious firm founded by his great-grandfather. Did someone actually try to kill Alex that day, or was it another one of his ruses? The answer was obvious.

On Monday, Sept. 6, Alex issued a statement through a Columbia public relations firm:

"The murders of my wife and son have caused an incredibly difficult time in my life. I have made a lot of decisions that I truly regret. I'm resigning from my law firm and entering rehab after a long battle that has been exacerbated by these murders. I am immensely sorry to everyone I've hurt including my family, friends and colleagues. I ask for prayers as I rehabilitate myself and my relationships."

After hearing Alex's sorry excuses, journalists sniffed and slobbered around Hampton like starving hounds in search of the tiniest bone of truth. What kind of rehab was Alex talking about? Almost everyone knew he drank a lot, but few were aware of his opioid use. Investigators had already surmised Alex was connected in some way to the murders of his wife and son. Now his law partners had gone public about missing money and ditched him. The state Supreme Court would surely suspend his law license and everyone questioned his story about being shot. Why wouldn't they be on him like a fly on a fried chicken wing?

Randolph "Randy" Murdaugh IV — the only family member still directly associated with the law firm — issued a statement:

"I was shocked, just as the rest of my PMPED family, to learn of my brother Alex's drug addiction and stealing of money. I love my law firm family and also love Alex as my brother. While I will support him in his recovery, I do not support, condone or excuse his conduct in stealing by manipulating his most trusted relationships. I will continue to pursue my clients' interests with the highest degree of honesty and integrity, as I always have."

A week later state law enforcement agents confirmed that an investigation had begun into allegations that Alex Murdaugh stole money from his former clients and the PMPED law firm. The next day Curtis "Cousin Eddie" Smith was arrested at his home near Walterboro in connection with shooting Alex alongside Old Salkehatchie Road. Some locals were known to claim friendship, or even kinship, to the Murdaughs regarding legal matters. Reporters had dubbed Smith "Cousin Eddie," and some people think he is Alex's actual relative, albeit a distant one. That's because family trees have tangled roots and limbs in rural South Carolina. Folks whose families have been around here for generations are likely to be related by blood, as in-laws or maybe both.

Regardless of who's who in the families, Alex had helped Smith with previous run-ins with the law. Smith had a police record but nothing serious was on it thanks to Alex. In return, when Alex needed someone to do him a special favor, he called on Curtis Smith — all on the sly, of course, thanks to attorney/client privilege.

The state charged Smith with attempting to help Alex commit suicide, assault and battery of a high and aggravated nature, and pointing and presenting a firearm in a conspiracy to commit insurance fraud for the benefit of Murdaugh's surviving son.

For Alex even more trouble arrived two weeks after the botched suicide. On Sept. 15, 2021, the state opened an investigation into the settlement of the estate of Alex and Maggie Murdaugh's housekeeper Gloria Satterfield, who had fallen down the front steps at Moselle and later died. The probe focused on the way $4.3 million from an insurance settlement was handled through her estate attorney Cory Fleming, Alex's former roommate at the University of South Carolina. Satterfield was at Moselle when, supposedly, she tripped over family dogs and fell down the front steps to the house. She was taken to the hospital, where weeks later she died. No autopsy was performed and her death was listed as "natural." Presumably, some folks in rural South Carolina consider tripping over a dog to be spontaneous.

Also that day, Alex's attorneys issued a bombshell statement about Curtis Smith's role in the botched suicide of their client:

"On Sept. 4 it became clear Alex believed that ending his life was his only option. Today, he knows that's not true. For the last 20 years there have been many people feeding his addiction to opioids. During that time these individuals took advantage of his addiction and his ability to pay substantial funds for illegal drugs. One of those individuals took advantage of his mental illness and agreed to take Alex's life by shooting him in the head. But Alex was not killed by the

gunshot wound. Alex is fully cooperating with SLED in their investigations into his shooting, opioid use, and the search to find the person or people responsible for the murder of his wife and son. Alex is not without fault, but he is just one of many whose lives have been devastated by opioid addiction."

However, "Cousin Eddie" Smith was already in police custody and singing a different tune. He told a *New York Times* reporter he was not involved in the life insurance scheme. He said Alex masterminded what happened and he (Smith) was a victim of Murdaugh. The following day Alex was hit with three criminal charges: insurance fraud, conspiracy to commit insurance fraud and filing a false police report. The state alleged Murdaugh had conspired with Smith in the botched killing attempt so Alex's surviving son, Richard Alexander "Buster" Murdaugh Jr., could collect $10 million in life insurance.

According to state investigators:

Smith was alone in his truck following Alex's Mercedes on a rural Hampton County road when Murdaugh pulled over to the side and got out of the car. Minutes later Smith drove up, pointed a pistol at Alex's head, pulled the trigger and drove off. Murdaugh received a glancing head wound and called 911. A helicopter was dispatched and airlifted him to a Savannah hospital. Investigators went to the spot where Alex had stopped and checked out his car. One of the tires was flat, apparently punctured by a knife, which they found in a ditch on the other side of Old Salkehatchie Road. It belonged to Alex Murdaugh. The shooting was staged.

Alex was treated for a head wound and reportedly checked himself into a rehab center. He turned himself in to authorities at noon on Sept. 16 and was booked into the Hampton County Detention Center. A bond hearing was scheduled that afternoon in magistrate's court. Meanwhile, a huge contingent from media organizations set up camp in the parking lot.

"What's Mr. Murdaugh's state of mind?" a reporter asked as defense attorney Harpootlian arrived.

"He's in the jail," Harpootlian replied. "That's his state of mind."

When asked if Murdaugh would go back into rehab if granted bond, Harpootian said, "I hope so," then went inside. Alex, wearing a green jumpsuit with HCDC on the back, shuffled into the courtroom and sat down. His wrists and ankles were shackled and chained.

Harpootlian told the magistrate that his client was neither a danger to the community nor a flight risk, adding the only violence he had committed "was against himself." He asked that his client be released on bond: "Alex has fallen from grace ... he is not a man of means anymore. He doesn't have the financial means to leave the country."

Harpootlian also said Alex had accepted responsibility for his crimes and would fully cooperate with SLED. "He detailed every element of what he is charged with today and wants to tell the truth." When Harpootlian said the recent murders of Maggie and Paul were the tipping point in his client's battle with opioid addiction, Alex cried and tried to use his shackled hands to wipe away his tears.

"Yes ma'am," Alex responded when questioned directly by Judge Tonja Alexander. She said he would be freed on a personal recognizance bond totaling $20,000 for all three charges against him, and that he must surrender his U.S. passport. Prosecutors had requested a $100,000 surety bond and that he wear a GPS monitoring device. The judge made no mention of GPS monitoring in her ruling. She did not ask Murdaugh what he intended to plea to the charges.

Murdaugh agreed to a waiver of his extradition because he planned to enroll in an out-of-state rehabilitation center. The facility was not made public at that time. After the hearing, Harpootlian was asked by a reporter, "Which state is the rehab center in?"

"None of your business — ever heard of that state?" Harpootlian responded.

"What's Alex's mental state?" another journalist asked.

"Mentally, not bad. Physically, he's been on opioids 20 years."

Harpootlian also said Curtis Smith had long been Alex's drug dealer. When asked if Alex and his wife had been having marriage troubles at the time she died, Harpootlian said, "Absolutely not ... always a picture of domestic bliss."

While Alex Murdaugh was in a Florida rehab facility clearing his head and body of the ravages of drug abuse, public suspicion gathered in dark clouds over those in charge of the three-month-old investigation into who murdered Maggie and Paul Murdaugh. Why had no one yet been charged?

Meanwhile, Murdaugh's public relations representative in Columbia issued the following statement in response to a national magazine article alleging Maggie had consulted a divorce attorney not long before she was killed:

"The recent allegations by *People Magazine* regarding the state of Maggie and Alex Murdaugh's marriage are totally inconsistent with what we have been told by friends and family members. Also, we have reviewed many years of text messages on Alex's phone, and the conversations between Alex and Maggie portray a very loving relationship. It is our hope that the media will continue to focus on covering the investigation of the person or people responsible for the murders of Maggie and Paul, and not reporting salacious stories with no credible sources connected to the Murdaugh family."

Alex was still in rehab in mid-October when SLED agents drove to Orlando, Fla., and returned him to South Carolina, where he was charged with two counts of obtaining misappropriated insurance settlement funds that were supposed to go to the sons of Gloria Satterfield, the housekeeper who fell down steps at the Moselle house and later died from her injuries.

The Satterfield family's attorneys, Eric Bland and Ronald Richter, told the *Greenville News*: "Today is a bittersweet day for the Satterfield and Harriot [Gloria's maiden name] families. They are extremely grateful to law enforcement, SLED and the South Carolina Attorney General's office for its investigation and today's criminal charges against Alex Murdaugh. The families and their attorneys are proud of how our justice system has conducted itself since the family had the courage to file its initial lawsuit on Sept. 15, 2021, detailing the theft of the money recovered for the heirs of Gloria Satterfield in connection with her death." The lawyers said the families had been betrayed by those they had trusted, and "their loved one's death was used as a vehicle to enrich others over their clients. The bottom line is no one is above the law."

A month later Alex Murdaugh was in a holding room inside the Lexington County Courthouse while outside, media crews had stretched huge cable cords from their trucks across on the courthouse grounds and lined a cement walkway with tents, lights, camera stands and other equipment. Inside Courtroom 3B, reporters with cellphones, laptops, cameras and microphones waited for Alex's bond hearing to start. Also there were state prosecutors, Murdaugh's defense attorneys and others.

Alex shuffled in wearing ankle restrains and handcuffs attached to a chain wrapped around his waist and bolted behind his back. He slouched a bit and held his head down as he fidgeted his fingers. This time he wore a dark-blue jumpsuit, orange shoes, black-rimmed glasses and a black covid facemask. He sat on the first row between his attorneys and soon began rocking his torso back and forth. As if on cue, everyone in the room got quiet. The only sounds were a multitude of clicks from reporters' cameras.

Murdaugh and his lawyers sat to the right of the room and a Richland County sheriff's deputy was in close proximity. Gloria Satterfield's sons and other members of the family were seated on the other side of the courtroom behind their attorneys. The Satterfields shared a quiet moment of prayer together prior to S.C. Judge Clifton Newman calling the hearing to order.

Attorneys Bland and Richter opened with an accusation that Alex Murdaugh had arranged an elaborate scheme to cheat the late Gloria Satterfield's two sons out of millions in money paid out by an insurance company from which he, Alex, had purchased a wrongful-death policy. They said that, soon after Gloria's death, Alex convinced her sons to hire Beaufort attorney Cory Fleming to help them sue the insurance company, and they were told the settlement money would be placed in a special holding account for safekeeping.

The sons' attorneys told Judge Newman that Alex did not tell them that Fleming was his close friend and former USC roommate. The attorneys also said Murdaugh was a danger to himself and others, noting he had recently arranged his own death to get a separate insurance payoff for his surviving son, but the attempt failed.

"We have never seen such a breach of trust: a man who stole money from the very family of the housekeeper that helped raise his kids," Bland told the judge. "Today is the day Alex Murdaugh needs to get comfortable being uncomfortable. He stole, he's a liar and a cheat."

The state's lead prosecutor, Creighton Waters, told the judge that the two new charges against Murdaugh represented only the tip of the iceberg in an investigation of a much broader case against him. Waters said that, in 2015, Alex Murdaugh, opened a personal account at Bank of America he tagged "Forge," which was easily confused with a highly respected holding company named Forge Consulting. Murdaugh had deposited clients' settlement payments into the account before diverting the money to himself, Waters said.

Defense attorneys Harpootlian and Griffin pointed out to the judge that Alex Murdaugh was a long-suffering victim of drug addiction overwhelmed by grief after finding the bodies of his wife and son. They said Alex had cooperated with the prosecutors, volunteered to submit to drug tests and turned himself in to face criminal charges.

Attorney Bland countered, asking, "If he's been an opioid addict for 20 years, how is it that he tried cases? How is it that he worked with judges? He is a clear and present danger to the citizens of this state."

Judge Newman refused to even consider a personal recognizance bond. "There is no amount of bond that the court can set which can safely provide protection to Mr. Murdaugh and to the community," he said before asking to see results of a psychiatric evaluation of the accused and ending the hearing.

Outside the courtroom, attorney Richter said, "the Satterfield family had some taste of justice today," adding he was convinced prosecutors would recover money owed to other victims of Alex Murdaugh's crimes.

Harpootlian later said rumors that Alex had been involved in the deaths of Gloria Satterfield and Stephen Smith were false, and that state authorities were responding to public pressure surrounding the investigations. He cited attorney-client privilege and declined to answer when asked if Murdaugh had admitted to masterminding the scheme involving the Satterfield settlement. Defense attorneys Harpootlian and Griffin left in a black Mercedes parked in front of the courthouse. Still shackled, Alex Murdaugh was placed in a police vehicle and taken to his new home — a tiny cell inside the Alvin S. Glenn Detention Center in Columbia.

21

BLACK FRIDAY

As the story of Alex Murdaugh gripped the nation, Lowcountry residents prepared for the Thanksgiving holiday, which for many included going on a shopping spree on "Black Friday." But Alex wasn't going anywhere. He sat in his prison cell under a dark cloud of suspicion.

He was indicted in the botched roadside shooting and insurance fraud scheme; accused of stealing millions of dollars from clients; kicked out of the family firm for finagling his finances; and still under investigation for possibly playing a role in the murders of his wife and son.

On Nov. 19, 2021, South Carolina Attorney General Alan Wilson announced that the state grand jury unsealed five state indictments against Alex Murdaugh. They totaled 27 criminal charges: four counts of breach of trust with fraudulent intent, seven counts of obtaining signature for property by false pretenses, seven counts of money laundering, eight counts of computer crimes and one count of forgery. These alleged crimes spanned several years against multiple victims in the Lowcountry. Among them were the sons and the estate of housekeeper Gloria Satterfield, who died after falling down the front steps of the Moselle house.

Eric Bland, an attorney for Gloria Satterfield sons, described the indictments as "Alex Murdaugh's version of Black Friday" and told reporters he was involved in the theft of a $4.3 million insurance settlement earmarked for his clients but never delivered. Murdaugh, who knew the sons, had advised them to file suit against himself and receive hundreds of thousands of dollars from his insurance company that was covering accidents at Moselle. Bland also said Alex had told the boys to contact Beaufort lawyer Cory Fleming (Murdaugh's former roommate at USC and close friend), who would arrange the payout.

Meanwhile, investigators uncovered evidence that the Satterfield conspiracy was only one of several similar frauds Alex had arranged. One of the state indictments alleged that Alex had used his prestige to swindle other clients in Allendale, Colleton, Orangeburg and Bamberg counties. One of his alleged victims was Thomas L. Moore, a highway patrolman injured in the line of duty. Moore had asked for help from Alex, who was accused of defrauding the patrolman and others of more than $4.8 million in payoffs. The S.C. Attorney General's Office acknowledged that the FBI and the U.S. Attorney's office were involved in the state indictments — which indicated that federal charges might be forthcoming.

Indeed, more charges rolled in like waves on a Lowcountry beach while Alex sat in a Richland County jail cell. On Dec. 9 the state grand jury issued seven more indictments against him for crimes in Hampton, Beaufort and Colleton counties. They included nine counts of breach of trust with fraudulent intent; seven counts of committing computer crimes; four counts of money laundering; and one count of forgery. These indictments outlined proposed schemes to defraud clients of almost $1.4 million. Among the victims was businessman Jordan J.J. Jinks, a Murdaugh family friend.

The following week Alex got another shot at getting out of jail on bond when he appeared before a grand jury for virtual hearing on the new charges. Creighton Waters, chief attorney of the state attorney general's grand jury division, argued that Murdaugh should remain behind bars because he was a drug addict, a danger to himself and others, had powerful family connections and had preyed on numerous trusting and vulnerable people. Waters said some of Alex's latest victims had identified themselves to authorities, and had since been harassed. He did not identify the victims or those said to have been harassing them.

Murdaugh's attorneys responded by citing Alex's apology to the Satterfield family and saying their client had agreed to sign a $4.3 million confession of judgment in their favor. Dick Harpootlian, Alex's lead attorney, noted that his client would not be a flight risk or able to commit crimes because he no longer had a law license, no clients and no means of stealing from anyone. He said Alex had become a different person since falling from grace, that he was no longer taking illicit drugs and could not afford a high bond.

Alex told the judge he had been addicted to opioids for 20 years, that he grieved the loss of his wife and son, and had felt his world caving in on him the day he was shot in the head. He admitted that he had hurt his family, friends and former law partners, and said his surviving son was "trying to be a lawyer, and is one of the best men I have ever known who deserves none of this." Alex also said he had humiliated his wife's family, "who were proud of me and my family's legacy … I made a terrible decision that I regret. I'm sorry and, quite frankly, embarrassed."

Alex told the judge he had been opioid-free for 98 days and had undergone 28 days of substance abuse treatment so far. He vowed to continue to do so. He said he was not a danger to himself. "My head is on straight now … I'm thinking clearer than I have in a long time. Your Honor, I have been humbled and surprised by the outpouring of love and support I have received … I want to repair as much of the damage as I can, and repair as many relationships as I can."

But Alex's sob stories and promises got him nowhere. State grand jury presiding judge Alison Renee Lee set a surety bond of $7 million with no option to make payments. This exceeded the amount requested by the prosecuting attorneys by $2.3 million. She said that if Alex did come up with the bond money, he would be held under house arrest with electronic GPS monitoring, mandatory mental health and substance abuse counseling, and random drug testing. She said he would not be allowed to contact witnesses, victims and co-defendants linked to any criminal cases filed against him. She stipulated that if Murdaugh required additional treatment in a residential facility, it must first be approved and located in South Carolina.

Murdaugh spent the Christmas holidays in the Richland County jail. On Jan. 4, 2022, his lawyers asked for a reconsideration or reduction of the bond. The requests were denied. Two weeks later the state attorney general announced issuance of four more grand jury indictments against Murdaugh, including 23 new charges: 19 more counts of breach of trust with fraudulent intent and four more counts of committing computer crimes. These charges alleged that Murdaugh had committed crimes starting in 2011. He was accused of carrying out criminal schemes that included funneling money through Palmetto State Bank in Hampton and using a fraudulent bank account at the Bank of America. Victims included the estate and family of Hakeem Pinckney, a deaf Hampton County man who had become a quadriplegic in a car crash and later died. Alex Murdaugh now faced 15 state grand jury indictments that included 71 charges and fraud that totaled $8.5 million.

Was it possible that Alex Murdaugh could have committed all these crimes on his own? An answer came on March 16, 2022 with four superseding indictments against Murdaugh and 18 charges against alleged co-conspirator Cory Fleming — the Beaufort lawyer who was Alex's former college roommate. The new charges were connected to the multi-million-dollar Satterfield fraud case.

Fleming's law license had already been suspended when he turned himself into authorities on the morning of March 17, and his bond hearing began within hours. State prosecutor Waters told the court that Murdaugh could not have defrauded the Satterfields of more than $4 million in insurance settlement proceeds without the assistance of Fleming, who had allegedly split the legal fees with Alex.

More charges were filed and additional accomplices were named when the grand jury issued three more superseding indictments, not all of them related to the Satterfield fraud case. They included 21 charges against Hampton banker Russell Lucius Laffitte, of another prestigious Lowcountry family, four against Alex Murdaugh and five against Fleming.

Laffitte, 51, had been chief executive officer of Palmetto State Bank. His job had been terminated in January after he was accused of using the bank to help Murdaugh misappropriate client funds held in trust. Laffitte had served as conservator for some of those clients. The charges against him included breach of trust with fraudulent intent and criminal conspiracy. Fleming was also accused of helping Murdaugh misappropriate funds from clients other than the Satterfields, and using client funds for personal expenses to take himself, Murdaugh and another attorney on a private plane to the 2012 College World Series in Omaha, Neb.

Laffitte turned himself in at the Kershaw County Detention Center on May 6 and had a virtual bond hearing the same day. He wore a pea-green detention center jumpsuit, and his wife, sister and other family members were with him. Laffitte, who did not enter a plea, answered direct questions from the judge. His lawyers asked the court to release him on his own recognizance or with a 10 percent cash-option bond. They said he was not a flight risk and posed no danger to the community. They also noted he was no longer employed by the bank. They described Laffitte as a community leader and lifelong Hampton County resident who would fully cooperate with investigators.

"As soon as he found out what Alex had done — and he was tricked — he tried to make one of the victims whole," Lafitte's defense attorney Bart Daniels told the court.

But Justin Bamberg, attorney for the late Hakeem Pinckney's family, reminded the judge that his client was a quadriplegic and some of the crimes occurred after he had died in a nursing home. "It was not as simple as white-collar stolen money," Bamberg said, adding that Lafitte demonstrated callousness and conscious disregard for his client.

The judge granted Laffitte a $1 million surety bond with a 10 percent cash option plus house arrest with electronic monitoring and other conditions. Laffitte was indicted for participating in schemes to defraud Pinckney and others of more than $1.8 million. Fleming was charged with helping defraud victims of more than $3.8 million.

Alex Murdaugh now faced a total of 82 criminal charges: 79 in state grand jury indictments plus three local ones. State attorney general spokesman Robert Kittle told *The Hampton County Guardian* that if Murdaugh was found guilty on all charges and maximum prison sentences were applied consecutively, his prison term would total more than seven centuries.

22

Lawsuits Galore

In the decades following Randolph Murdaugh Sr.'s death in 1940, the law firm that became PMPED (now Parker Law Group) — a personal-injury giant in Hampton, S.C., was known as a self-proclaimed friend of the little guy against mighty corporations. It humbled corporate adversaries, including CSX Transportation, the forerunner of which ran the train that hit and killed Randolph Sr. near Almeda.

PMPED filed four dozen personal injury cases against CSX between 1992 and 2002, and the train company had paid $18.8 million in verdicts and settlements, according to a *Forbes* magazine article titled "Home Court Advantage." Most of them involved railroad accidents in cases filed in the Hampton County Court of Common Pleas. Under state judicial venue laws at that time, if a company such as CSX owned property or did business anywhere in Hampton County, personal injury suits could be brought in Hampton no matter where in South Carolina the incident occurred. Cases filed in Hampton were advantageous to the Murdaugh firm because jurors were local and generally compelled to favor local lawyers and award larger-than-average totals for damages.

The firm also helped bring major reforms to railway and other transportation laws and practices that saved innumerable lives. Lawsuits filed by the firm's lawyers enhanced its ever-growing reputation. Murdaugh family members joked about their legacy. "A train killed my grandfather in 1940, and they have been killing our people ever since," Randolph Murdaugh III quipped in 2018 during a speech to locals.

Legal reformists challenged South Carolina's tort and venue laws in the late 1990s, and specifically named the 14th Judicial Circuit as extremely favorable to lawyers who file personal injury suits.

In 2004 the American Tort Reform Foundation listed Hampton County as the third worst "judicial hellhole" in the nation for such activities. The ranking was based on the number of out-of-county injury cases filed in

Hampton and the amounts victims got in settlements and judgments.

Forbes reported that in the year 2000 Hampton's reputation for having an anti-corporation legal environment was directly responsible for Walmart's decision not to build a store in the county. Principle PMPED partner John E. Parker dismissed the notion as propaganda. *Forbes* quoted him as promising not to sue any similar big-box retailer that moved to Hampton, and offered to represent such companies free of charge. None took him up on the offer.

However, by February 2005 the Murdaugh mystique was fading. The S.C. Supreme Court had issued a decision that changed the state's venue laws aimed at eliminating law firm venue shopping. This limited the number of out-of-town cases brought back to Hampton and ended the gilded era for the Murdaugh-founded law firm.

In 2022 Alex Murdaugh was drowning in lawsuits, both criminal and civil, filed against him. The first wave included an initial wrongful-death suit filed in Beaufort by Mallory Beach's mother, Renee. She blamed her daughter's death on Gregory Parker and Parker's Corporation, which owned a convenience store that sold beer and hard seltzer to underaged Paul Murdaugh; Luther's Rare and Well Done Bar and Grill that sold liquor shots to Paul and Connor Cook; and James and Kristy Woods, the Hampton County couple who owned the river house where the oyster roast was held.

Renee Beach's original suit did not name anyone in the Murdaugh family. She later filed a lawsuit in Hampton County against Murdaugh Residence Trust 2, Richard Alexander Murdaugh, Richard Alexander Murdaugh Jr. and Randolph Murdaugh III, individually and as a trustee of the Murdaugh Residence Trust 2. This wrongful-death suit was amended several times after Randolph III died and as certain parties resolved charges.

One by one, each boat-crash survivor filed suits as well. On July 7, 2021, survivor Connor Cook filed a pre-suit discovery petition against the S.C. Department of Natural Resources, the Beaufort County Sheriff's Office and "unknown others" to gather evidence, including cellphone records and depositions from several of the law enforcement officers who had worked the boat crash. Cook's lawyers said the actions were necessary to "confirm or refute evidence of a civil conspiracy of their client." They maintained that there was an effort to misdirect the criminal investigation away from Paul Murdaugh and place the focus on Cook. In addition, Cook's attorneys filed a civil suit alleging civil conspiracy against multiple parties, including

Alex Murdaugh.

On Sept. 15, 2021, Bland Richter LLP, representing the Gloria Satterfield estate and her two heirs, filed suit against Alex Murdaugh alleging he had conspired with others to steal her death settlement and insurance monies.

On Oct. 6, PMPED sued Alex Murdaugh to recover money missing from the firm, its partners and clients. Alex, as a law partner, had developed a systematic scheme in which he diverted funds owed to the firm and to clients to a fictitious banking entity that he controlled. The suit alleged that for several years Alex submitted false documentation to the firm and to clients that allowed him to funnel stolen funds into fraudulent bank accounts. The lawsuit also sought discovery on where the money went and if any remained hidden. In addition, the firm inquired as to whether Alex had entered into any agreements that involved future payments related to books, interviews or other publicity.

On Oct. 28, Alex's older brother and former law partner, Randolph "Randy" Murdaugh IV, filed a suit to collect $46,500 he had loaned to Alex but had not been repaid. The next day, law partner John Parker filed a suit claiming that Alex owed him $477,000 in unpaid personal loans. Within two days, Alex's attorneys filed confessions of judgement on both debt-collection lawsuits, acknowledging that Alex owed the money and stating he would not contest the debt in court — an action which would have allowed Murdaugh's former partners to be paid before any of the other victims. Outraged, attorneys for the others soon filed motions to stay those confessions of judgement.

Before the end of the year, the remaining boat-crash survivors filed suit. On Dec. 2, 2021, Keith Anthony Cook sued for injuries he sustained in the crash. On Feb. 15, 2022, Miley Altman and Morgan Doughty each filed a personal-injury lawsuit related to the crash. Both women were represented by Allendale attorney Mark Tinsley, who also represented the Beach estate.

All of these lawsuits were filed in state civil courts. In May, 2022 an amended version of a federal lawsuit was filed in U.S. District Court by the Nautilus Insurance Company, which had paid out claims in the 2018 death settlement of Gloria Satterfield that were allegedly stolen. Named as respondents in the suit were Alex Murdaugh; suspended Beaufort attorney Cory Fleming and his former law firm of Moss & Kuhn, P.A.; and Hampton County banker Chad Westendorf and his bank of employment, Palmetto State Bank. The Nautilus company is an Arizona-based insurance carrier that had provided a $5 million umbrella insurance package to Alex and alleged it also was a victim of fraud and conspiracy, adding "the scope of Murdaugh's depravity is without precedent in Western jurisprudence."

On June 2, 2022, a civil lawsuit was filed against Alex Murdaugh, former banker Russell Laffitte and Palmetto State Bank of Hampton. It was a personal-injury suit filed in Allendale County Court of Common Pleas by attorney Mark Tinsley on behalf of Arthur Badger and the estate of Donna Badger, who was killed in a 2011 crash involving a UPS truck. The suit alleged that Murdaugh and Laffitte, through the services of Palmetto State Bank, conspired to steal settlement funds from Arthur Badger, who was Murdaugh's client at the time, and from the estate of his late wife. Murdaugh was a partner at PMPED, the law firm built by his ancestors, and Laffitte was the vice president and then CEO of Palmetto State Bank, founded by his family more than a century ago. The firm and the bank were among the most prominent businesses in the Lowcountry.

On Oct. 7, 2022, a suit was filed in Hampton County Court of Common Pleas on behalf of Manuel Santiz-Cristiani, a citizen and resident of Chiapas, Mexico and a former Murdaugh client who had been injured in a 2008 car accident on Interstate 95. The suit named Alex Murdaugh and PMPED; Palmetto State Bank and Laffitte; Ronnie L. Crosby, a PMPED partner and shareholder; and William F. Barnes III, a former PMPED associate. Crosby and Barnes filed actions seeking to remove their names from the suit because they said they had nothing to do with Alex's actions.

By then Alex was directly named in 12 civil suits — 11 state and one federal — and he was connected in some way to several related lawsuits. His financial accounts were frozen and his assets seized and placed under control of two court-appointed receivers at the request of Tinsley and the Beach estate. The idea was to appraise then sell Alex's homes and real estate parcel by parcel to pay as much as possible back to his victims, pending the outcome of the multitude of civil cases. Alex Murdaugh was snared in an interlocking web of criminal and civil cases alleged to have occurred in several S.C. counties. At the center of it all was Hampton — the "judicial hell hole" turned sink hole in which Alex had no way of escaping. Yet still, in his drug-muddled mind, he thought there was a way out.

23

A FULL CUP OF JUSTICE

HAMPTON COUNTY, January 2022 —

State Grand Jury indictments against Alex Murdaugh mounted and what seemed to be a long, multicounty crime spree of the former deputy solicitor with the famous last name was shocking. How many more victims were there, and where did all the money go? How much, if any, would each victim get back? How much did Alex have left to his name, and was he hiding any ill-gotten assets?

In response to such questions, Beach family attorney Mark Tinsley told *The Hampton County Guardian* that "all the victims are entitled to justice, but you can't get blood from a turnip." As the Beach case and other Murdaugh-related lawsuits slogged through pre-trial processes, an initial measure of justice emerged as an apology and a promise of financial recompense for the Satterfields. The family's attorneys had filed the first version of their personal injury suit against Murdaugh et al. on Sept. 15, 2021. Various parties initially involved in Alex's insurance scheme against the late Gloria Satterfield's estate were quickly settled and dropped from the suit.

No one wanted to be on the same side of the table with Alex Murdaugh, Satterfield attorney Eric Bland told the newspaper. By January 2022, the Bland and Richter firm had recovered more than $7.5 million in settlements for the Satterfield estate and Gloria's children, Brian Harriott and Tony Satterfield. But they squeezed nothing from Alex Murdaugh.

"The Satterfields are doing well, and they feel they have gotten almost a full cup of justice," Bland said. "The house has fallen for Alex Murdaugh … much has taken place by them coming forward. This case has accomplished a great deal. On a personal level, they (their clients) feel some sense of satisfaction for helping clean up a system that has been broken for quite some time. This case was the hub, everything else spoked out of it. I said that this was going to take down Alex Murdaugh, and it did. It got the ball rolling. We kind of got SLED, the FBI, everybody directing their attention to this whole slew of financial crimes ..."

During a Dec. 13, 2021, bond hearing, Murdaugh's attorneys read part of Alex's apology to the Satterfields and said he had agreed to a $4.3 million confession of judgment in their favor. But it would take a court hearing along with several months of negotiations with Murdaugh and his attorneys with the court-appointed receivers and other interested parties to make that official and legally binding. On May 16, 2022, Judge Daniel Hall filed an order in Hampton County Court of Common Pleas allowing Murdaugh to sign the confession of judgement, and it was filed in Hampton County court two weeks later. It was signed by Alex Murdaugh and Gloria's two sons. By this judgment, which was now legally enforceable, Satterfield's sons are the first unopposed judgment creditors of record against Alex.

In typical passionate and flamboyant Eric Bland style, a news release stated that the judgement was both meaningful and symbolic for several reasons. "As we all recall, after the lawsuit was filed by Gloria's estate, Mr. Murdaugh denied liability for the $4.3 million stolen from the estate of Gloria Satterfield after Gloria fell to her death on Feb. 2, 2018, on the stairs of the Moselle property. Thereafter, Mr. Murdaugh had the audacity to advance the preposterous notion that he owed no money because the estate collected in excess of $7.5 million from others, including Cory Fleming; his law firm Moss, Kuhn, and Fleming; PMPED and Palmetto State Bank from claims asserted against them. By this judgment, Mr. Murdaugh admits that the allegations contained in the complaint against him are true and admits that he stole the $4.3 million in settlement funds that belonged to Gloria's estate."

This sad saga was nearing the end for Gloria's family, the statement added, as they awaited the outcome of the co-receivers' efforts in collecting money and property from Murdaugh and others. With $7.5 million in settlements already won, the Satterfields and their attorneys also announced they would use a portion of the settlements and the confession of judgement to form a charitable foundation in Gloria's honor to benefit underprivileged Hampton County families — "good God fearing, law abiding and hardworking people like Gloria who struggle to make ends meet will be the beneficiaries of this foundation," said Bland and Richter. "As we have said all along, Gloria did not die in vain. Her death now had a purpose."

24

LAWYER TURNED DRUG DEALER

FITS News, founded by Will Folks in Columbia, had delved into the morass of Alex Murdaugh's past and published a story in 2021 about his connection to the late commercial fisherman Barrett T. Boulware of Allendale, who was a suspect in the Lowcountry's infamous Operation Jackpot smuggling operation a half-century ago:

Alex's grandfather, Solicitor Buster Murdaugh, was a contemporary of Barrett Boulware's father, Judge Thomas Boulware of Allendale. They had been co-counsels in 14th Judicial Circuit civil cases in 1949 and 1951. In the 1970s Barrett Boulware and his father were accused of using their fishing boats in the Operation Jackpot ring. This was in the early days of President Reagan's highly touted "war on drugs." Charges against both Boulwares were dropped after a key government witness was run over by a car in Florida and killed.

FITS News reported that Alex Murdaugh had been Barrett Boulware's legal representative with power of attorney. Probate records show the Boulwares owned several parcels of property, including some small Beaufort County islands. They also show that the Moselle hunting tract had belonged to Barrett Boulware, who was terminally ill and died. The Moselle property had an airplane hangar and short airstrip, which were rumored to have been part of Boulware's drug-smuggling operation.

Interestingly, in October 2021 anonymous sources told *The Post and Courier* and *The State* newspapers that the state grand jury was looking into the possibility that Alex Murdaugh was working with a violent Walterboro drug gang known as the Cowboys. On June 28, 2022, the state grand jury unsealed indictments of Alex Murdaugh and Curtis "Cousin Eddie" Smith, charging them with criminal conspiracy and narcotics-related crimes in connection with the Cowboy gang. While Murdaugh's earlier admission that he had been a long-time drug addict surprised many locals, the new indictments indicated that Alex was more than a victim of opiate dependence, as his attorneys had claimed.

Murdaugh and Smith were indicted on two conspiracy counts that included the illegal sales of the narcotic Oxycodone in the Lowcountry. In addition Smith was indicted for money-laundering, forgery, trafficking methamphetamine, unlawful possession of a Schedule II controlled substance and possession of marijuana. The indictment stated that between Oct. 7, 2013 and Sept. 7, 2021, Murdaugh, Smith and "other persons known and unknown to the grand jury," purchased and distributed Oxycodone. Smith was also indicted by the Colleton County Grand Jury on Nov. 18, 2021 for possession of methamphetamine with intent to distribute, and possession of marijuana.

The joint indictment accused Murdaugh and Smith of conspiring to commit financial crimes from 2013 to early 2021, during which time Alex wrote Smith at least 437 checks totaling $2.4 million, with the understanding that the latter would convert the checks into cash for Murdaugh to use in a myriad of unlawful activities.

Nearly all the checks were written for less than $10,000, which banks are not required to report to outside authorities. Murdaugh drew the checks on accounts at multiple banks and made them payable to various versions of Smith's name as well as Smith's daughter and another woman thought to be his girlfriend. According to the indictment, Smith forged their signatures on the back of the checks and cashed them at the Enterprise Bank of South Carolina in Walterboro. A story written by John Monk of *The State* newspaper referred to Smith as Alex Murdaugh's "money mule."

Prior to announcing the charges, Smith was arrested and booked into the Colleton County Detention Center where officials could keep an eye on him and, perhaps, get him to talk about his dealings with Murdaugh.

On Aug. 19, 2022, new indictments mentioned more illegal activity about Murdaugh including charges he stole money from his older brother and law partner Randolph "Randy" Murdaugh IV. Two additional names were identified as possible drug-ring associates.

Alex Murdaugh was charged with four counts of obtaining signature or property under false pretenses, three counts of money laundering and two counts of computer crimes. On Dec. 16, 2020, he allegedly stole $91,868 from his law firm by having a client's check deposited into a fraudulent account created under the name of "Richard A. Murdaugh Sole Prop DBA Forge." On May 12, 2021, Murdaugh allegedly stole another $83,333 using the same method. A third indictment alleged that, through false representations, he received a loan repayment for $121,359 from the firm that was supposed to go to his brother Randy.

These indictments named Spencer Anwan Roberts and Jerry K. Rivers as Murdaugh's criminal accomplices. Roberts was accused of conduct involving narcotics, dangerous drugs, or controlled substances among other charges. Rivers was charged with one count of obstruction of justice for allegedly taking a cellphone belonging to a suspect that had been arrested on Aug. 10, 2020, in connection with multi-county drug crimes.

At that point Alex Murdaugh was accused of defrauding victims of almost $8.8 million and a total of 97 criminal charges and possible jail time totaling as much as 700 years. But investigators and journalists kept digging. On Sept. 10, 2022, *The New York Post* published a story saying Murdaugh accomplices Rivers and Roberts were in fact members of the Walterboro Cowboys gang. A *Post* reporter quoted an anonymous member of the gang who said, "Alex Murdaugh is running half the drugs in Colleton County."

25

FALL FROM GRACE COMPLETE

RICHLAND COUNTY, S.C., Jan. 4, 2022 —

It was Alex Murdaugh's turn to use the pay telephone in the Alvin Glenn jail, and he had to hurry. Each prisoner had 10 minutes before the call would be disconnected. Alex's younger brother, John Marvin Murdaugh, was on the line, and his call was being monitored and recorded:

Alex: *"Have you talked to Randy (oldest brother Randolph IV) since ... last week?"*.

John Marvin: *"Yeah, I talked to him, umm, I talked to him yesterday,"*.

Alex: *"Okay."*

John Marvin: *"You know about the law firm, don't ya?"* John Marvin asked.

Alex: *"No."* (His voice changed tone slightly, as if he was braced for more bad news.)

John Marvin: *"Yeah, the law firm has dissolved, and they are reforming under a new name."*

Alex: *"I didn't know nothing about that. What is that?"*

John Marvin: *"Yes, because of all the negative publicity and all the stuff they're going through."*

Alex: *"What is the new name?"*

John Marvin: *"Um they ... It's going to be operated under the Parker Law Group."*

Alex: *"The what?"*

John Marvin: *"Parker Law Group."*

Alex paused: *"10-4."*

John Marvin: *"And I think it's a LLC partnership, or LLP, in each partner's name, and operates under the 'Parker Law Group' heading."*

Alex: *"I hate they're having to go through all that."*

John Marvin: *"Yeah, they catching ... They going through all kinds of stuff."*

Alex: *"Is anything I can help with?"*

John Marvin sounded as if he stifled a laugh: *"Naw, man…"*

That was when Alex learned that the legendary family law firm, founded by his great-grandfather in 1910, had dropped the Murdaugh name. The partners announced the name change on Jan. 4 "in honor of John E. Parker, of Hampton, for 50 years of outstanding service to PMPED." Randolph "Randy" Murdaugh IV was the only founding family member still with the firm.

It is interesting to note a small headline in the Oct. 10, 1973, edition of *The Hampton County Guardian* saying, "4th Generation Murdaugh in Court." The story reported that five-year-old "Alec" Murdaugh was on duty that Monday during Hampton County General Sessions Court to draw names for a jury panel, just as his father had done when he was a child. Alex's grandfather, Buster Murdaugh, was solicitor at the time and his father, Randolph III, was assistant solicitor. Young Alex had officially become the fourth generation of the family to take part in Hampton County's courthouse proceedings.

Being an attorney and a prosecutor was the goal of each Murdaugh man who followed in Randolph Sr.'s footsteps. It was their tradition, their identity, their claim to fame. It represented the sum total of their pride. But for Alex, the middle son of the third Randolph Murdaugh, pride was stripped away on July 12, 2022 when the S.C. Supreme Court disbarred him from practicing law in the Palmetto State. Alex's grandfather, Buster, was threatened with disbarment in the 1950s, but managed to get off. Alex was the first and only Murdaugh to experience the ultimate judicial sanction.

The state Supreme Court considered Alex's own admissions of committing crimes and other acts before demanding his disbarment. Alex had "admitted to conduct that amounts to clear and convincing evidence of dishonesty …," according to the ruling. While Alex had neither entered a formal plea on any charges nor been tried and convicted of any crimes, the justices' decision was based on his confession during bond hearings that he was liable and responsible on more than one occasion for participating in criminal activity. His defense lawyers, Harpootlian and Griffin, did not try to fight his disbarment.

Since being jailed in the Alvin S. Glenn prison in Columbia in October 2021, Alex's phone conversations had been recorded by authorities. Reporters

Mandy Matney and Liz Farrell of *FITS News* filed freedom of information requests for copies of his calls and the newspaper published them in June 2022. They included conversations between Alex and his family members about prison life, football and Alex's success gambling with other inmates. They were playing to win beef-sticks from the prison canteen.

On Feb. 28, 2022, Murdaugh's lead attorney Harpootlian filed a "complaint for injunctive relief" in federal court requesting a halt of the release of Alex's phone calls, but it was rejected. *FITS News* had also obtained Alex's jailhouse commissary shopping list and published it online under the headline: "Can't afford underwear? $4 Mayonnaise? Alex Murdaugh's Commissary Receipts Tell Different Story." The story's subhead said, "Also, he's been moisturizing ..."

Reporter Farrell used S.C. Freedom of Information open-records requests to obtain Alex's commissary receipts and deposit slips. The article poked fun at comments Harpootlian had made during previous bond hearings about his client's assets being frozen, therefore he did not have enough money for clean underwear or to purchase mayonnaise. The article detailed every purchase Murdaugh had made while in jail, as well as who gave him the money to do so. It included the size and type (boxers) of Murdaugh's underwear and that other items included lip balm and petroleum jelly.

The Murdaugh name continued to fall from grace when, on May 4, attorneys for Morgan Doughty, one of the 2019 fatal boat-crash survivors, filed a five-page affidavit in the Hampton County Court of Common Pleas citing numerous incidents of Alex and his family's alcohol abuse, including parental tolerance for underage drinking by their children and friends.

It stated that Morgan Doughty was Paul Murdaugh's longtime girlfriend who had spent numerous hours with him and his family. It said she had first-hand knowledge of Paul's alcohol consumption as well as his parents' knowledge and facilitation of their son's heavy drinking. The affidavit alleged that Paul consumed alcohol almost daily and often was grossly intoxicated while driving family-owned trucks and a boat. It claimed that his parents knew about it, were often present, and provided alcohol to Paul and his underage friends. One photo in the affidavit is of a bikini-clad girl on a boat pouring an alcoholic drink into Alex's mouth. Others shots showed Paul drinking alcohol in the presence of adults.

By then news and social media throughout the English-speaking world were reporting stories and photos featuring Alex and the murders of his wife and son. Alex was mocked in memes and taunts on Twitter, and his face was featured on a T-shirt under which was printed, "Don't trust your soul to no backwoods Southern lawyer," from a Reba McEntire song.

There seemed to be no privacy for Alex Murdaugh now, and he had yet to be charged with murdering his wife and son. It wasn't until July 14, 2022 — more than a year after the killings — that the state announced indictments against Alex Murdaugh. The Colleton County Grand Jury charged him with two counts of murdering Maggie and Paul and two counts of possession of a weapon during the commission of a violent crime. It said Alex killed Maggie with a semi-automatic rifle and Paul with a shotgun. No other details were included. Murdaugh attorneys Griffin and Harpootlian denied the murder allegations in a statement released minutes after the charges were announced:

"Alex wants his family, friends and everyone to know that he did not have anything to do with the murders of Maggie and Paul. He loved them more than anything in the world. It was very clear from day one that law enforcement and the Attorney General prematurely concluded that Alex was responsible for the murder of his wife and son. But we know that Alex did not have any motive whatsoever to murder them."

SLED Chief Mark Keel also issued a statement:

"Over the last 13 months, SLED agents and our partners have worked day in and day out to build a case against the person responsible for the murders of Maggie and Paul and to exclude those who were not. At no point did agents lose focus on this investigation. From the beginning I have been clear: the priority was to ensure justice was served. Today is one more step in a long process for justice for Maggie and Paul."

Parker Law Group posted the following statement:

"Today's news is sad and upsetting. Our thoughts turn to Maggie and to Paul, whom we loved and we miss. Every day we grieve for them. Justice must be served. If the charges reported today are true and just, we ask for our judicial system to act swiftly and bring a conclusion to this heinous situation."

Murdaugh's bond hearing for the murder charges was July 20 in the

Colleton County Courthouse in Walterboro. Alex, handcuffed with reading glasses perched atop his close-cropped haircut, wore khaki pants and a white dress shirt. He pleaded not guilty to the charges. When asked how he wished to be tried, Murdaugh replied with a traditional legal phrase: "By God and my country," indicating he wanted a jury of his peers to decide his fate. His lawyer, Harpootlian, added, "We would like to get this matter before a Colleton County jury as soon as possible so Alex can get this behind him and so SLED can look for the real killer."

The trial date was scheduled for Jan. 23, 2023, setting the stage for what became the most watched criminal trial in South Carolina history. It would be held in the same Colleton County courthouse where Alex's grandfather, Solicitor Randolph "Buster" Murdaugh Jr., was accused of accepting a bribe in a headline-grabbing moonshine conspiracy trial. A portrait of Buster glared down from a back wall of the crowded courtroom where his grandson Alex stood while being denied bond for the murders.

PART THREE

26

A Trial by 'God and Country'

"We don't have to prove shit!" Alex Murdaugh's attorney Dick Harpootlian responded to a query prior to the Jan. 23, 2022 start of the double-murder trial in Walterboro. Indeed, proving Alex gunned down his wife and son within moments using both a shotgun and semi-automatic rifle was a tough assignment for the prosecutors. Prior to the start of the trial, prosecutors said they would not pursue the death penalty against Murdaugh — which suggested their case was weak. He faced a maximum sentence of life in prison with no chance of parole.

Judge Clifton Newman had denied bond for Alex, who was already jailed on 106 other criminal charges for which he could not pay a $7 million bond. Observers were surprised when the judge issued a pre-trial gag order on everyone involved in the murder case after he had promised the proceedings would be open to the press and public. Judge Newman also ordered removal of a portrait of Alex's late grandfather — former 14th Circuit Solicitor Buster Murdaugh — from a wall of the Colleton County Courthouse.

Approximately 900 jury duty notices had been sent to Colleton County residents, and the state published a list of 255 possible witnesses. Officials from the Colleton County Clerk of Court's office and the city of Walterboro started early to prepare for a massive influx of visitors to the quaint town near Interstate Highway 95 known as "The Front Porch to the Lowcountry."

Additional police officers began arriving days before the start of the trial to help local cops secure downtown Walterboro. Soon a city-within-a-city of TV trucks, recreational vehicles, food trucks, a media center for reporters, and rows of what locals considered "luxury porta-potties" enveloped courthouse square. News organizations and others had rented virtually every available square foot of office space. Tents popped up everywhere, fiber optic cables carpeted sidewalks, lights stole the darkness, and aromas of fresh-cooked food from trucks permeated the air. A media circus had come to town and center stage was in the courtroom under the metal roof of the 203-year-old courthouse.

The roughly 900 potential jurors reported to the courthouse in four groups. They would be carefully screened and narrowed down to 12 jurors and six alternates. Attorneys from both sides asked each candidate the usual questions. Almost all said they had heard or read about the Murdaugh murders, and many knew Alex Murdaugh and/or members of his family. A few said they had direct connections. The attorneys questioned each, huddled, then asked another, huddled, and so on. It was like watching National Football League team owners figuring out who to draft first and who to select later. Two days of wrangling passed before a panel of 12 jurors and six alternates were sworn in. Each would be paid almost $20 per day, five days a week, to sit in judgment of Alex Murdaugh. None appeared enthusiastic about the task.

Observers gathered each day before dawn outside the courthouse. Journalists and others with proper identification were allowed to enter upon arrival. They sat among a courtroom filled with crime sleuths, authors, lawyers and others. Walterboro Mayor Bill Young created a stir after someone said he was the bestselling author John Grisham. Each day well-dressed Alex Murdaugh, with an arm full of files, took his seat up front with his defense team. During breaks he spoke with his lawyers. He flashed a cocky smile intermittently as if he were there for a client's hearing, not on trial for killing his wife and son. While the jury was out of the room, lead defense attorney Harpootlian walked around chatting and joking with other lawyers.

But the prosecutors looked determined, while stern-faced officers from the Colleton County Detention Center stood stiffly near Murdaugh, a reminder that "Big Red" was in serious trouble.

Siblings Randolph "Randy" Murdaugh IV, John Marvin Murdaugh and Lynn Goette sat near the front of the courtroom behind Alex, whose surviving son, nicknamed "Buster" after his great-grandfather, sat a few feet behind the defense table with his aunt and uncles. During breaks Alex spoke briefly with his family members or simply turned and mouthed, "I love you" to them. The warm and fuzzy feelings melted away in time.

Opening statements began on Jan. 25 as dark clouds gathered over Walterboro. The lead prosecutor was Creighton Waters — a University of South Carolina law school graduate, short in stature and feisty like a gamecock, the USC mascot. He proved himself an effective orator, opening with a detailed description of the "catastrophic damage" suffered by Alex's wife and son. He stressed that neither body showed signs of defensive wounds — that they knew their killer and were not alarmed initially.

Waters' voice rose as he told the jury that Maggie and Paul Murdaugh were shot at close range, then exclaimed "Pow! Pow!" Buster's Aunt Lynn jolted upright in her seat. Waters continued: "The evidence will show malice afore-thought, and that malice existed for a while in the mind of Alex Murdaugh." At that moment a hard rain began pounding the courthouse roof. Waters proceeded to describe a perfect storm of trouble, deceit and death that had gathered, then he turned, pointed at Alex Murdaugh and thundered, "He was the storm and the storm arrived on June 7, 2021." Outside the courthouse great sheets of rain were falling.

Waters' opening statement was brilliant. He highlighted evidence he said would prove Alex Murdaugh was a charlatan and habitual liar who had murdered his wife and son. Waters asked the jury to listen carefully as the evidence was explained. He advised them to watch Alex's facial expression as the facts unfolded, and especially during recorded interviews with police. Use common sense when considering what you hear and what you see, Waters recommended to each of them before he gathered up his notes and sat down.

Defense attorney Harpootlian opened saying it was an honor to represent his friend Alex Murdaugh, who he asked to stand up and face the jurors. "This is the loving father of Paul and the loving husband of Maggie," Har-pootlian said, adding that the state's case against his client was based on illogical theories, not facts. He reminded the jurors that Alex was innocent until or unless proven guilty.

He said Paul was the apple of Alex's eye, then launched into a lurid descrip-tion of the young man's brain injuries. One of the shotgun blasts "literally exploded his brain, like a watermelon … shot to hell," he declared. No loving father was capable of such carnage, he said, as Alex hung his head and wept.

Harpootlian questioned the credibility and accuracy of the prosecution's evidence. He trashed what he called theories of motive, and pointed out that police did not have a murder weapon, any eyewitnesses or other direct evidence. He questioned the prosecution's timeline for what happened the night Maggie and Paul died. He said two shooters killed them, not one. "They (investigators) decided that night that Alex did it … and they have been pounding that same square peg into a round hole for quite some time. But he did not do it. He didn't kill — butcher — his son and his wife, and you need to put out of your mind any speculation that he did."

As the trial went on jurors were shown photos and videos taken at the murder scene. Judge Newman sealed the more gruesome visual evidence. Computer screens were covered with cardboard so that only jurors could see it, not members of the audience. Opening testimony centered on Alex's 911 call that fatal night and his interactions with medical responders and local police officers who arrived first at Moselle. Among them was Sgt. Daniel Greene, a bearded Colleton County deputy and detective with close-cropped hair and a no-nonsense attitude, who told the court what he saw while securing the crime scene.

As he described Paul's body face down in pools of blood and water on the cement floor of the kennels' feed room, Alex slowly rocked his torso forward and back while seated at the defense table. Several rows behind him, his brother John Marvin grimaced then wrapped his arm around Alex's visibly shaken surviving son Buster, who was sitting next to his uncle.

Sgt. Greene's body-cam video was entered into evidence. It recorded the deputy's initial interaction with Murdaugh, who suggested the killings might have been linked to Paul and the fatal boat crash on Archers Creek. The deputy's camera also recorded Alex as he described finding the bodies of his wife and son, and checking each for a pulse. Alex said he found them that night soon after returning from a visit with his mother in Almeda. Alex offered Sgt. Greene his cellphone, which documented specific times he had earlier called Maggie.

Alex had told the dispatcher that, not long after he found the bodies, he went to the Moselle house, grabbed a shotgun and returned to the scene in case the killers were still around. Sgt. Greene took the loaded Benelli Super Black Eagle 12-gauge shotgun as evidence. Greene testified that Murdaugh appeared upset and nervously anxious. In the body-cam video, the jurors saw and heard Alex sniffling, crying, breathing heavily — then stopping intermittently to greet passing officers and others to say, "How ya doing?" The video also showed a dead chicken on top of a dog crate in the kennels.

Capt. Angela Stallings, who oversaw Colleton County's 911 center among other duties, testified that emergency calls are recorded, and an unredacted copy of Murdaugh's call was played in the courtroom. Alex is silent while the phone rings. When the dispatcher answers, he begins breathing heavily and appeals for help. He tells the dispatcher that, when he arrived in his truck at the kennels, he saw the bodies and checked each for a pulse. He repeatedly tells the dispatcher that his loved ones did not kill themselves. He mentions the boat crash in Beaufort and threats made to Paul. He says the last time he spoke to his wife was about two hours before he found the bodies.

As the jury listened to the 911 recording, prosecutor Waters stood briefly and pumped his clenched fist as if he was celebrating a touchdown. Most observers did not know why.

Capt. Jason Chapman, a 26-year veteran of police work, was called to the stand as an expert witness for the prosecution. Chapman looked sharp in his dress uniform and said he had testified in numerous trials, including federal cases. He said several things about the Murdaugh case seemed odd: Paul's body was face down across a concrete walkway in front of the door to the feed room and next to the dog cages; Paul's body was covered in blood mixed with water; his hands were under his body; and his cellphone appeared to have been placed near a back pocket.

According to Chapman, Alex told authorities he had checked Paul's pulse and his son's phone fell out of a pocket, and that Alex picked up the device and placed it on his son's back. Chapman testified that what Alex had said about checking the body for a pulse was odd because Paul's wrists were under his body, did not appear to have been disturbed and no blood was on Alex's hands or clothes. He said Paul's cellphone had no traces of blood on it.

Chapman testified it was not clear how Maggie and Paul had gotten to the kennels. Did they walk from the house that muggy evening? Did they drive over in a car or golf cart? He also noted that Alex's emotions and body language were erratic when questioned.

Sgt. Dothan Varnadoe, of the Colleton sheriff's department, tested Murdaugh's hands for gunshot residue at the crime scene. He said hands and clothes appeared to be clean: no dirt, no debris, no blood. Sheriff's detective, and SLED liaison, Capt. Laura Rutland testified that Alex had said he touched both his wife and son's bodies that night. But she saw no blood on him, on his shoes or his clothing, which had smelled freshly laundered. She said she also checked the areas around the bodies and saw no knee prints or foot prints.

Did Alex lie about checking the pulses of his wife and son? Did he change clothes after finding their bodies? Prosecutor Creighton Waters underscored these questions then asked Capt. Rutland, "Is the individual who told you twice that he tried to roll Paul over and check his pulse — the individual who was clean from head to toe — present in the courtroom?"

"Yes," she replied.

Defense attorney Jim Griffin suggested Alex was clean because he didn't kill them. Griffin asked Rutland about strands of brown hair found on Maggie's hands. Alex's hair is red, he said, suggesting the brown hair belonged to her actual killer. The defense team's tactics were clear in cross-examinations of each officer and special agent. The goal was to cast reasonable doubt that Alex killed his wife and son, and to raise questions about the quality of their investigations: Why wasn't the scene properly preserved? Why were Murdaugh's friends and law partners allowed to trample the site? Why weren't footprints or tire tracks given proper attention? Why didn't State Law Enforcement Division agents do a thorough search of the Moselle house?

SLED forensics agent and criminologist Melinda Worley is a brunette of slight stature who reminded some observers of FBI agent Clarice Starling's character in the film "The Silence of the Lambs." Worley testified that she took custody of spent rifle casings, gunshot residue, knee and shoe impressions near the bodies and clothes Murdaugh was wearing that night. She used computer software and evidence gathered at the scene to show flight paths of the rounds fired from a rifle and shotgun like those believed to have been the murder weapons. She offered a scenario showing how one shooter could use both weapons to kill the victims.

Defense attorney Harpootlian began his cross-examination of her with an insult: "What's so special about a special agent?" He also questioned each of Worley's conclusions, then offered a counter theory for each one. "One explanation is there were two shooters, correct?" he asked. Worley said, "Yes."

He asked about unidentified footprints found at the scene, and why investigators did not preserve evidence inside the feed room. He said too many people had been allowed to go inside the room. "Do we know what other evidence they may have destroyed?"

At times Harpootlian performed like the veteran trial lawyer he was reputed to be. At other times he seemed confused and mumbled like an old man who had lost his car keys. At one point Harpootlian fumbled about searching for items he wanted to enter as evidence, prompting Judge Newman to ask if he and his defense team needed more time to prepare.

Harpootlian made a name for himself decades earlier when he successfully prosecuted serial killer Donald "Pee Wee" Gaskins. In the Murdaugh case, Harpootlian's co-counsel Griffin made a more significant impact on the jury.

Silver-haired SLED Special Agent Jeff Croft had been a cop longer than most of his fellow officers had been alive, and his experience was evident on the stand. Croft, who had taken into evidence firearms and ammo from the Murdaugh residence, testified that live, 147-grain S&B 300 Blackout rounds found inside Moselle's gunroom and Blackout casings picked up from the shooting range and in a nearby flower bed were the same brand and weight as the spent rifle casings found around Maggie's body. Croft also said state agents found spent 12-gauge shotgun shells around the property that matched the weight and manufacturer brand as those found near Paul's body. He said SLED had seized several Murdaugh family weapons capable of firing those rounds.

However, when prosecutors tried to present the weapons into evidence, defense attorney Griffin objected. While the ammo might match the guns, he said, neither had been proven to be the actual murder weapons. Judge Newman overruled Griffin's objection.

Prosecutors then played a video of SLED Agent Croft's interview with Murdaugh three days after the murders. Alex told investigators that Paul had been careless with his guns, often leaving them around unattended, and added that his son's custom-made 300 Blackout rifle was missing, probably stolen from his truck. Alex also said on the tape that the last time he saw Maggie and Paul was when they had supper earlier that afternoon inside the Moselle house. The jurors viewed Alex weeping as he described a ride he had taken earlier with his son around the Moselle property.

On the video agents tried to comfort Alex, and handed him facial tissue to wipe away his tears. As Alex watched the video in the courtroom, he rocked back and forth while seated at the defense table and grabbed a tissue for his eyes and nose. Later in the recorded interview Alex said something that got everyone's attention. Did Alex, between sobs while describing his son's horrific wounds, tell Croft, "I did him (Paul) so bad?" Or did Alex say, "They did him (Paul) so bad?"

Croft testified he was "100 percent confident" that Alex had said, "I did him so bad." But Murdaugh's attorneys were quick to dispute this, saying Alex had said, "They did him so bad." Was it or was it not an unintended confession of guilt? The judge agreed to replay the video for the jury. It was difficult for observers seated in the courtroom to determine Alex's exact words. Some said they heard "I" while others heard "they."

The trial continued with the state calling John Bedingfield, a S.C. Department of Natural Resources officer and custom gunmaker who happened to be a Murdaugh relative. Bedingfield testified that between 2016 and 2018 he built three AR-style, 300 Blackout caliber rifles for the Murdaughs, and he had been told that one of them was missing from the family arsenal. Was the missing rifle used in the murder?

Throughout the trial the state called cellphone forensic experts from Verizon Wireless as well as others who worked as agents for SLED. Most of their testimony was technical and confusing. That changed when SLED Lt. Britt Dove took the stand. He identified himself as a supervisor in the state's computer crimes division who also served on U.S. Secret Service and FBI computer-forensics task forces. He testified that he had extracted cellular data from cellphones that had belonged to Alex, Maggie and Paul. He said he had retrieved text messages, call logs, the number of footsteps each user took while holding the devices and various updates of the phones.

Dove said early on the day Maggie died, she was at the Edisto beach house and texted a friend that Alex had asked her to come to Moselle. Dove said data showed several phone calls were made and erased that day on Alex's cellphone prior to the murders. He also testified that data showed Alex had called several people that night, including five missed calls to Maggie's phone between 9:04 p.m. and 10:03 p.m., prior to dialing 911 and reporting he had found the bodies.

Dove said data from Maggie's phone showed a text message to her was opened at 8:49 p.m. It had been sent by "Lynn G." — Alex's sister, Lynn Murdaugh Goettee. Maggie's phone became locked soon afterward and remained inactive. Dove testified that Paul's phone showed no significant activity after 8:50 p.m., which was odd because Paul was a habitual user day and night. Dove also noted that Alex's phone showed no activity for roughly an hour until minutes after 8:50 p.m., and that whoever was holding it took 283 steps, more than what had been registered all day.

Dove said iPhone passcode protection on Paul's phone had blocked SLED from opening stored data for almost a year until state and federal forensics experts cracked it. They did a full extraction of the phone's files and found a critical piece of evidence: Paul had made a live video of a call from the kennels at 8:44 p.m. to his friend Rogan Gibson. The video was of Gibson's dog Cash, which Paul was keeping in the kennels. Paul was talking in the background about Cash as the video showed an injury to the dog's tail. Also audible were the voices of Maggie and a man who sounded like Alex. They were talking about one of the Murdaugh family's dogs, which at that moment had a dead chicken in its mouth.

Until that point all of the evidence was circumstantial. But this video along with voices of Alex and Maggie were recorded by Paul only moments before he and his mother were gunned down. A collective gasp filled the courtroom. This evidence was a bombshell. Was it really Alex's voice? Was he there when Maggie and Paul were killed?

Alex looked like a man staring into the headlight of a runaway train. He began rocking his torso forward and back while nodding his head up and down. He had sworn to God and everyone else that he did not kill his wife and son. He had vowed to all he was with his mother at her home in Almeda at the time when Maggie and Paul were murdered. He had claimed that the last time he saw his loved ones alive was hours earlier during an early supper at Moselle after which he took a nap, then drove straight to Almeda and back. Upon his return, he called 911 and told the operators he had found the bodies of Maggie and Paul. He told authorities the same thing on numerous occasions. His attorneys had filed a pretrial notice of alibi stating that Alex Murdaugh was never at the kennels that night until after he had returned from his mother's house and found the bodies.

On Feb. 1, 2023 during the second week of his double-murder trial, a video taken by his youngest son moments before he died blew Alex's alibi all to hell.

Grief and anguish defined Rogan Gibson's demeanor as he walked to the witness stand. He did not want to be there. He was a lifelong friend of both Paul and Buster; Maggie was another mother to him; the Murdaughs were his second family. He had already told police he had been talking on the phone to Paul that night, and mentioned he heard what sounded like Alex's voice in the background. But this was not confirmed until more than a year after the murders — when investigators finally cracked the codes on Paul's locked phone, saw the video and heard the audio. Gibson met with the investigators in November 2022 and saw what Paul had recorded but did not send to him the night he died: In effect, Paul was testifying from the grave. He had filmed his friend Rogan's brown Labrador retriever, and zoomed in on the dog's injured tail. Then Maggie's voice emerged from the background along with that of a man yelling at the Murdaughs' dog Bubba, another retriever, which had a bird in its mouth. "It's a dead chicken," Paul said.

As Gibson sat on the stand in the packed Colleton County Courtroom, he knew what state prosecutors were about to ask him. Rogan knew whose voice he heard admonishing Bubba. He knew Alex's voice when he heard it.

"Did you recognize the voices of your second family — Paul, Maggie and Alex Murdaugh?" prosecutor Waters asked Gibson while Paul's audio/video recording played in the courtroom.

Gibson said they were the voices of Paul, Maggie and Alex Murdaugh.

Are you sure? the prosecutor asked.

"I'm 100 percent sure," Gibson responded.

If this was true, Alex Murdaugh's voice confirmed he was at the murder scene at 8:44 p.m., five minutes before both Paul's and Maggie's cellphones locked down. There was little doubt now that between 8:44 and 8:49 that night, Alex's wife and son died in a hail of gunfire from two distinct weapons. It was obvious at that point to almost everyone in the courtroom that Alex had lied about when he left Moselle that evening and he was at the scene when his wife and son were murdered.

Defense attorney Jim Griffin cross-examined Rogan Gibson, and asked about the boat-crash lawsuit and threats against Paul following Mallory Beach's death. He elicited from Gibson only positive comments about Alex's character. Griffin did not mention that Alex appeared to have been caught in a lie about not being at the murder scene moments before the killings.

As the trial continued the jury heard testimony from numerous Murdaugh family friends, associates and employees. They included Paul's friends Nathan Tuten and Will Loving, both saying they were sure the third voice on the recording was Alex's. In addition Loving said that, in the spring of 2021, he and Paul had set the sights on the missing 300 Blackout AR as they stood on Moselle's gunroom porch — months after Alex told authorities the rifle had been stolen. Loving also said Paul had sent him a Snapchat video taken earlier on the day of the murders showing Alex wearing different clothing than what he had on when police arrived at the scene that night. Tuten testified that, after the killings, Alex had told him Paul's death meant he (Alex) could beat the boat case lawsuit and clear his late-son's name.

All the while Murdaugh's attorneys steadfastly attempted to block negative evidence and similar information about Alex and pertaining to the lawsuit from being entered into the record. Curiously, they also tried to block testimony about Alex's alleged financial crimes. But Judge Newman had not yet ruled on the admissibility of such matters. Griffin's line of questioning about the boat-crash case was a crucial misstep for Alex's defense.

"You have opened the door..." the judge told Alex's lawyers, adding he would hold in-camera hearings (which means without the jury present) to receive evidence related to the boat crash lawsuit and the alleged financial crimes, then rule on its admissibility before the jury.

While the jurors were out of the courtroom, victims, lawyers, bankers and others testified about what they knew regarding Murdaugh's alleged financial crimes. They described how Alex had used his family name and connections to help pull off his schemes. The judge was told that when Alex was caught moving money around, he would tell his partners he had made honest mistakes before being allowed to make things right as a legacy partner in the firm's system of unity and trust.

Palmetto State Bank's new CEO Jan Malinowski testified that when Alex's account experienced an overdraft, Murdaugh, although he already owed millions, received "possibly the most generous overdraft policy ever seen." Malinowski had replaced Palmetto State's disgraced Russell Laffitte, who had been generous when handling accounts connected to his life-long friend Alex Murdaugh.

One victim of misappropriated money was another one of Alex's friends from childhood, Chris Wilson, who had his own Bamberg law firm. Wilson's testimony was emotional, almost pitiful for observers in the courtroom, about Alex's betrayal:

"He was one of my best friends, and I thought he felt that way about me ... I had loved the guy for so long. I probably still love him, but I was so mad." Wilson said Alex lied to him and stole legal fees that belonged to the Bamberg firm. As Wilson spoke, Alex hung his head and wiped away tears.

PMPED managing partner Ronnie Crosby testified at that time and said the Murdaugh murders had shut down for months the firm's inquiries about Alex's suspicious activities, thus giving him some time to cover some of his tracks.

At one point prosecutor Waters rose and told the court, "When the hounds are at the door, when Hannibal is at the gates for Alex Murdaugh, violence happens," in reference to the roadside shooting on Old Salkehatchie Road. "They (the jury) really need to understand what this man was hiding."

Murdaugh's lawyers had scoffed at the notion that a man would commit murder to distract from lesser crimes, especially because Alex had numerous other options. But Waters countered, saying Murdaugh was a desperate man who knew that the boat-crash lawsuit would expose a decade of his malfeasance. He said Alex was a master manipulator who tried to make it look as if his own family members were victims of murderous vigilantes upset by the death of Mallory Beach. He said Alex thought the Beaches' wrongful death suit would be dropped, giving him more time to hide his crimes and replace the stolen money.

After listening to one witness after another, Judge Newman ruled that lawyers from both sides could plead their cases in relation to Alex's alleged financial crimes before the jury. The ruling extended the trial and allowed more evidence regarding Alex's financial dealings and other questionable activities.

After the jury returned to the courtroom, PMPED's chief financial officer, Jeannie Seckinger, was the first witness called to the stand. She was bitter, convinced that Alex had been stealing money from the firm and his clients for years, and angry he had made her look either complicit with his crimes or incompetent. Alex violated the trust and brotherhood of the firm, she said, and testified in detail about how she thought money was stolen by Alex from the firm, his clients and even his older brother. She did not sugar-coat her words. Reporters later joked that if they took a shot of whiskey every time she used the word "stole" while cutting her eyes at Alex, each would be in an alcohol-induced coma before the next court recess.

Seckinger told the jury she confronted Alex about missing legal fees on the morning of the shootings, which prosecutors had already described as part of the perfect storm that led Alex to kill his loved ones, try to get sympathy from others and distract from his litany of financial and other crimes.

SLED Special Agent Paul Greer looked and talked like a soft-spoken science teacher, not a firearms and ballistics expert who had tested thousands of weapons and testified in 25 state and federal criminal cases in his long law enforcement career. He was seated in the Murdaugh trial despite Harpootlian's protest about the accuracy and reliability of his testing techniques.

Greer told the jury that firing pin dents and other marks on spent 300 Blackout AR shell casings near Maggie's body matched those of older used casings from the same weapon found elsewhere on the Moselle property. "Only one 300 Blackout rifle made those markings," he testified, and it was missing. Alex had earlier told authorities that Paul's 300 Blackout had been stolen prior to the murders. Green said the marked casings found at the murder scene matched those previously fired elsewhere on the property. In other words, the tests indicated that Paul's missing rife was used to kill his mother.

Agent Greer's tests of the two spent shotgun shells used to kill Paul were less conclusive. Alex had in his possession a 12 gauge Benelli Super Eagle automatic shotgun when police arrived at Moselle the night of the murders. Alex told the officers that after he found the bodies he went to the Moselle house gunroom and returned with the Benelli for protection in case the killers were still around. Green testified that two spent shotgun shells found near Paul's body matched in brand and size numerous other empty shells found elsewhere on the property. Greer also testified that he found traces of Maggie's DNA in blood on the Benelli that Alex was holding that night when police arrived. But Greer also said he was not 100 percent certain the same shotgun was used by Paul's killer.

Several days of mind-numbing financial testimony followed. Jurors appeared to lose interest as they watched the courtroom clock. One alternate appeared to be napping as she held a blanket over her face. Another was permitted to "dip" tobacco while sitting in the jury box and spit discreetly into a bottle or cup.

Week three got off to what could have been a bang — someone called in a bomb threat that emptied the courtroom; a deputy sprinted across the courthouse grounds while yelling for everyone to clear the area. The entire courthouse and the square were vacated for most of day 13 of the trial while a bomb squad searched the area. At around 3 p.m. the search was completed and authorities announced it had been a hoax unrelated to the Murdaugh case. It was, however, a stark reminder that anything could happen.

Mushelle "Shelley" Smith was next called as a witness. She was a caregiver for Alex Murdaugh's mother, Libby, who lived at Almeda. Alex had told investigators that he had left Moselle late on the afternoon of the killings and visited with his ailing mother. Smith, a long-time employee of the family, was nervous and emotional on the stand.

She testified about working as Libby's caregiver for years, and said she loved the Murdaugh family. She said she feared that her testimony might cause her to lose her job. She confirmed that Alex visited Almeda the night of the killings but only stayed at the house for 15 to 20 minutes. Smith also mentioned that Alex might have been trying to coach her prior to the trial by suggesting to her he had been at Almeda for 30 to 40 minutes, and he had offered to help pay for her own upcoming wedding.

In addition, Smith testified that about a week after the killings Alex arrived at the house unusually early in the morning and had something wrapped in what seemed to be either a blue vinyl tarp or blue rain jacket. After being questioned by the defense, she said she was not exactly sure if the object was in a tarp or a jacket.

Surprisingly, state investigators did not search the Almeda house for months following the murders. When they did on Sept. 16, 2021, they seized a blue tarp and a blue raincoat from the house. Tests showed the raincoat had significant amounts of gunshot residue both inside and out. Was Alex wearing this raincoat at the time of the shootings? Did he wrap the murder weapons inside the raincoat and later move them?

As prosecutors prepared to call Beach family attorney Mark Tinsley to the stand, Murdaugh attorney Phil Barber tried to block the effort. Barber told the court that a GoFundMe account had been established for Murdaugh caregiver Shelley Smith, and that among the first donations was a gift from Mark Tinsley. Barber said money contributed to the account would help Smith in the event that she lost her job for speaking up. Barber said Tinsley's name had been removed from the GoFundMe webpage, but that he did indeed donate money to a person who would testify as a witness for the prosecution, and therefore had a vested financial interest in the Murdaugh murder case.

Judge Newman disagreed. "That would be good fodder for cross-examination," he said, adding "I won't attempt to screen testimony in advance.

Lawyers ask questions, lawyers object, judges rule."

By the following Friday the GoFundMe account had received more than $20,000 in donations from a variety of people, a few with a sense of humor. One identified himself as a Murdaugh attorney and another was listed as "Fake Forge," in reference to the account with a misleading name through which Alex was alleged to launder millions in ill-gotten money.

Tinsley, who had been on Murdaugh's tail for more than two years, took the stand and detailed his efforts to pressure Alex into settling the Mallory Beach wrongful death suit. A trial would require Alex to disclose all of his financial assets. Tinsley said it was hard to believe that Murdaugh wouldn't settle, and even harder to believe Alex's claims that he was broke. Tinsley said a civil hearing on the boat case had been scheduled for June 10, 2021, but the murders three days prior to that had resulted in its cancellation. "Pretty quickly I realized that, if there was a vigilante involved, the suit against Alex Murdaugh would be over. If Alex is the victim of a vigilante, no one is going to hold him accountable, no matter what he did... Alex knew this."

Another conflicted witness called to the stand was Blanca Turrubiate-Simpson, also a longtime housekeeper for Alex and Maggie. Turrubiate-Simpson said she felt deep loyalty to the Murdaughs before testifying that Maggie told her that she and her family were worried about the multimillion-dollar boat-crash case. Turrubiate-Simpson also testified Alex had asked both his wife and Paul to make a special trip to Moselle on the day of the murders. She also described what Alex wore earlier that day before the murders, adding she never saw the clothing at Moselle or anywhere else afterward.

Turrubiate-Simpson said Alex asked her to go to Moselle on the morning after the murders and straighten up the house (still considered part of the crime scene). She also said Alex attempted to influence what she should say if police asked her about what he had been wearing on the day his wife and son were killed.

"I felt confused at first," she said. "I know what he was wearing when he left the house (to go to work) ... It didn't feel like he was inquiring what clothes he was wearing. It felt like he was trying to convince me of what clothes he was wearing."

On day 15 of testimony Judge Newman denied a defense motion for a mistrial then sent the jury out of the room amid a flurry of objections. Harpootlian's request for a mistrial came after prosecutor John Meadors asked

Turrubiate-Simpson if Maggie sounded anxious about the way Alex had handled family money matters. The judge overruled Harpootlian's objection, saying Meadors' question was fair game. Newman said testimony about the Murdaughs' finances and a relationship was pertinent, especially after Harpootlian had called witnesses who said Alex and Maggie were loving parents of a family free of serious internal squabbles.

Alex Murdaugh's paralegal, Annette Griswold, who questioned what appeared to be stolen legal fees and brought it to the firm's chief financial officer's attention, testified she had received text messages from Alex while he was away in the substance-abuse rehabilitation facility. She said Alex admitted in the message that he was addicted to drugs and was reckless in his behavior. "The worst part is I did the most damage to the ones I love the most," Alex wrote in the message.

Dr. Ellen Riemer, a Medical University of South Carolina forensic pathologist, performed autopsies on both Maggie and Paul Murdaugh. After being questioned by Murdaugh's defense attorneys, a feisty Dr. Riemer, who had qualified as an expert forensic witness in more than 250 previous criminal cases, responded by saying although Harpootlian and his team might disagree with her findings, "that doesn't change the truth."

Riemer described the victims' wounds in graphic detail. She pointed out which wounds did "catastrophic" damage and which were "immediately fatal." She described how Paul's brain had been "ejected" from the right side of his head — that his body arrived at the medical university hospital in one container and his brains, collected from the floor and walls of the feed room, were in another. She said neither Maggie nor Paul had wounds that appeared to be defensive. She said this indicated that each was caught by surprise, then outlined her findings regarding the angle, range and trajectory of rounds that caused each victim's wounds.

When photo exhibits included graphic photos of the bodies, one juror clutched her mouth and gasped. Most Murdaugh family members in the courtroom could not see the exhibits. Alex, seated between his lawyers at the defense table, did not look at the pathologist while she testified. He simply resumed his emotional routine of rocking the top half of his body back and forth. Was Alex expressing emotion or guilt, or simply putting on an act?

Witness Marion Proctor looked a lot like her younger sister Maggie Murdaugh. They were close in age, had a very close relationship throughout their lives and had no other siblings. Marion was stoic in her testimony until she described her sister's "sweet, free spirit." She also said Paul was "a sweet boy who had been misrepresented by the media." Marion said the fallout after the boat crash was devastating to both Maggie and Paul, and many of their friends and others in Hampton had turned their backs on the Murdaughs. She also testified that Maggie had told her that Alex asked her to come to Moselle on the day of the murders because he was especially worried about his father's failing health.

"You encouraged her to go to Moselle?" prosecutor Waters asked. "I did," she replied then broke into tears, saying it was the last time she spoke to her sister. Marion also said Maggie worried about Alex's fidelity and his drug use. When asked if she thought Alex could have killed his wife and son, she did not answer directly, saying Alex once told her that whoever killed them "had thought about it for a really long time."

Marion testified about other things that seemed odd to her. Why didn't Maggie go with Alex from Moselle to his parents' house in Almeda? That was why Alex had asked her to drive from the Edisto beach house to Moselle earlier that day. Marion also thought it strange that almost immediately after finding the bodies, Alex seemed more concerned about the boat-crash lawsuit, which was filed against him. She also said Alex seemed to be more concerned about getting his son Buster reinstated into law school than finding the killers of Maggie and Paul. "He (Alex) said his number one goal was clearing Paul's name," Marion testified as she looked through tears at Alex, "but my number one goal was finding who killed Maggie and Paul."

Under cross-examination, Marion she said her entire family had lived in fear of the killer or killers. Earlier, Murdaugh family members and some of the law partners testified that they were on high alert and worried for the safety of Alex, Buster and others close to them. But, she said, only Alex didn't seem to be worried or fearful.

SLED Senior Special Agent David Owen, who had previously interviewed Murdaugh several times, was called to the stand, and noted the following contradictions:

— On the afternoon of the murders Alex told investigators he left his office in Hampton about 5:30 p.m., drove 9.6 miles to Moselle, rode around the property with Paul for two hours, had supper with his wife and his son, and last saw them alive at 8 p.m. inside the main house, not at the kennels.

But investigators had confirmed that Alex was still at his office after 6 p.m. that afternoon.

— Alex told investigators he arrived at his mother's house a few minutes after 9 p.m., stayed 45 minutes to an hour, returned to Moselle, found the bodies near the kennels, checked their pulses and called 911 (at 10:07 p.m.). However, Shelley Smith, who looked after Libby Murdaugh at the house in Almeda, had testified Alex arrived later (9:22 p.m.) than he had said, and left after only 15 to 20 minutes.

— The last video on Paul's phone was taken at the murder scene starting at 8:44 p.m. and ended at 8:45. It showed that Alex was at the kennels with Maggie and Paul moments before the killings. Agent Owen noted the video taken earlier in the day showed Alex was wearing different clothes than what he had on when authorities arrived that night. Owen also said Alex had told investigators he was certain none of the family's dogs were out of the main house that night. However, Paul's video had recorded the voices of Alex and Maggie, who were talking about the dead chicken Bubba had in its mouth.

— Local, state and federal authorities had been investigating the case for two years and the only credible suspect they had was Alex Murdaugh.

Dr. Kenneth Lee Kinsey is an anomaly — a country cop with a PhD., an expert crime-scene forensic investigator and an educator as comfortable knocking down doors on a SWAT team as teaching students in a classroom. Kinsey had investigated an estimated 800 death scenes. He calmly addressed the court in a soft-spoken Southern accent reminiscent of a Sunday school teacher at a local Baptist church.

For the Murdaugh case, Kinsey's job was to study the autopsy results and crime scene evidence then show jurors precisely how Maggie and Paul were murdered. With grace and confidence he made sense of technical testimony and evidence previously presented to the jury. He described how and where each died, the range and trajectories of each round that ripped into their bodies and other gruesome details. He stood his ground when grilled by Murdaugh's defense attorneys, and jurors obviously were impressed.

Kinsey's testimony clearly supported previous testimony that Paul and Maggie were killed by one person who first killed Murdaugh's son using a shotgun, then the wife with a rifle — as if two people committed the murders. As Kinsey described the pain the victims experienced before dying,

Alex hunched over at the defense table and cried. During cross-examinations, Kinsey solidly defended his conclusions, making the defense seem foolish, even drawing laughs from courtroom observers.

Also earlier in the investigation, a General Motors representative told investigators the company retrieved very little information from the "black box" on Alex Murdaugh's Chevrolet Suburban. But after the nationally televised trial got underway, GM's legal department contacted SLED and offered additional information. What they found was stunning:

— Digital evidence from the black box provided a timeline of the Suburban's location and movement starting moments after the killings to Alex's mother's house at Almeda, and back to Moselle that night. Maggie's and Paul's phones went silent at 8:49 p.m. When combined with existing evidence, data showed that Alex's vehicle was cranked up at 9:06 p.m., traveled at a high rate of speed 13.4 miles to Almeda and stopped 23 minutes later behind his mother's house near some outbuildings. Was this when and where Alex first hid the murder weapons?

— Moments later the truck was moved next to the house, where Alex knocked on a side door and entered. Twenty-nine minutes later, at 9:45 p.m., Alex was back in his truck and returning to Moselle.

— The Suburban arrived at the kennels at 10:06 p.m. No one born and raised in the Lowcountry and in their right minds would speed up to 80 miles per hour on a dark, two-lane highway through woods full of wild deer. But that's what Alex Murdaugh did on the night his wife and son were murdered. In addition, the prosecution noted that Alex could not have checked both Maggie's and Paul's pulses in the twenty seconds that elapsed between the time he arrived at the scene and the time he called 911.

For almost two years following the June 7, 2021 slayings, investigators searched for the murder weapons in swamps, ponds and rivers on and around the huge Moselle hunting retreat. It was not until September 2023, after the data from Alex's truck was entered into evidence, that they searched the woods and swamps behind Libby Murdaugh's house at Almeda. By then, weapons and other evidence that might have been hidden on the property were not found.

27

FROM REAPER TO WEEPER

State prosecutors rested their case against Alex Murdaugh on Feb. 17, 2023 after four weeks of presenting findings from their deep dive into his motive. They included audio and video evidence of him at the scene moments before the murders, and his odd behavior afterward. The prosecution also offered powerful evidence of Alex's lies, theft of money from his clients and law partners, and what appeared to be a botched attempt to stage his own death on a lonely road to buy time to cover up financial crimes.

Murdaugh's defense team worked hard to discredit the work of state and local police and create doubt in jurors' minds that Alex killed his wife and son. They called to the stand Alex's brother John Marvin Murdaugh as well as Alex's surviving son, Buster. Both expressed love and loyalty to Alex, however their testimonies did little to change the course of what unfolded. Neither did testimonies for the defense from a handful of expert witnesses who charged as much as $600 an hour in consultation fees.

Alex's attorneys theorized that two gunmen, each only around 5 feet, 2 inches tall, killed Maggie and Paul. They offered ballistics they argued was proof that Alex, who stood more than 6 feet tall, could not have possibly done it — all of which prosecution expert Dr. Kenny Kinsey later described as preposterous.

The Murdaughs of old built the family's reputation on social standing, power politics and courtroom theatrics: Solicitor Randolph Murdaugh Sr. had forced a former governor to stand in the prisoner's dock; Solicitor Randolph Murdaugh Jr. once wrapped a garden hose around his neck, stretched out on the floor in front of the jury and pretended to be a murder victim; Solicitor Randolph III blurted out timely, humorous comments during trials that made the accused or their defense attorney look foolish.

Now, deep into the fifth week of his own double-murder trial, Alex Murdaugh opted to take the stand in his own defense. That was risky business. Harpootlian, his lead attorney, strongly advised Alex not to testify and sat quietly pouting while co-counsel Jim Griffin told Judge Newman that Murdaugh wanted to personally set the record straight about his finances. The judge approved the request. Alex stepped up to the stand, swore to tell the truth, sat down and started explaining:

— He testified that he had been addicted to painkillers for 20 years, initially to relieve lingering pain from a knee injury from playing football.

— He admitted that he stole money from clients and lied to many people.

— He vowed he had nothing to do with killing his wife and son. He wept while looking directly at each juror. He referred to his wife as "Mags" and his late son as "Paul Paul" — nicknames he had not used in recorded interviews with SLED.

While the Internet erupted with social media users mocking Murdaugh for this, Griffin asked Alex point blank, "Did you blow your son's brains out?" Through tears Alex responded: "I would never intentionally do anything to hurt either one of them." He steadfastly maintained that he had an early supper inside the Moselle house with his wife and son that afternoon, took a nap on the couch, drove to Almeda to check on his mother, returned to the Moselle house around 10 p.m. and later found his loved ones' bodies near the kennels.

During cross-examination, prosecutor Creighton Waters took no pity on Murdaugh. "Why did you lie to your clients?" he asked. "Why did you lie to the jury?" Why on more than one occasion Alex looked into the investigators eyes and said he was trying to help them find the killers, when actually he was not?

Alex tried to brush everything off, saying he could not remember all the details about what he had said and done that hurt others through the years.

Waters was relentless. "I know you want to get through this quicker, but we're not." He thumped a huge file of evidence stacked on the prosecutors' desk.

Alex hesitated momentarily, then said, "There were plenty of conversations where I looked people in their eyes and lied to them."

The prosecutor again showed the audio/visual video Paul had recorded at the kennels minutes before he and his mother were gunned down. It included Maggie's and Alex's voices. A silence enveloped the courtroom.

That's when Alex admitted he had lied to everyone for 20 months about his whereabouts moments before the murders. He said his addiction to opioids had clouded his thinking, creating in his mind extreme distrust of police. "As my addiction evolved over time, I would get in these situations, these circumstances, where I would get paranoid thinking. 'Oh, what a tangled web we weave'," he testified. "Once I told a lie — I told my family — I had to keep lying."

Alex proceeded to offer a revised account of what happened that night:

— After supper Alex rode with Maggie in a golf cart from the house to the kennels to see Paul.

— Soon after arrival, he and Maggie wrestled a chicken from the mouth of the family's Labrador retriever named Bubba. (That's when Alex's voice is heard calling the dog's name in Paul's video, along with comments by Maggie.)

— He quickly returned to the Moselle house in the cart, then drove his truck more than 13 miles to Almeda, where he visited his ailing mother.

— He drove back to the Moselle house, but no one was there, so he drove to the kennels, saw the bodies, checked their pulses and called 911 (received 10:07 p.m.).

Alex paused briefly during his testimony and sobbed. Then he looked directly at the jurors and said, "It was so bad." He said Paul was face down, and he had tried to roll over his son's body to check his pulse. "I could see his brain on the sidewalk. I didn't know what to do." He said he also checked his wife's body, which was a short distance away near a corner of the shed. Alex repeatedly referred to his youngest son as "Paul Paul" and to his wife as "Mags" as he eyed the jury and, intermittently sobbed and wiped his eyes and nose.

Alex told the jury his wife and son were murdered by others, not by himself. He said the killings were sparked by a steady flow of comments on social media about the deadly Beaufort boat crash, two years earlier, in which young Mallory Beach died. "I believe then and I believe today that the wrong person saw and read all that. I can tell you for a fact the person or people who did what I saw on June the 7th … They hated Paul Murdaugh, they had anger in their hearts."

On cross-examination, prosecutor Waters continued to press Alex: How was it possible that vigilantes knew Paul and Maggie would be at the kennels alone on June 7, and also knew Alex would not be there between 8:49 p.m. and 9:02 p.m.? He also asked Alex about the series of unanswered phone calls he started making to his wife and son at 9:02 p.m., after no activity was detected on his phone for nearly an hour. Was Alex's original alibi something an experienced lawyer and volunteer prosecutor would craft to show he was not the killer?

Alex responded: "I never manufactured any alibi in any way, shape or form because I did not and would not hurt my wife and my child ... I did not kill Maggie, and I did not kill Paul. I would never hurt Maggie, and I would never hurt Paul ... ever!"

Murdaugh knew he had been skewered about what Waters described as Alex's "new story" of what happened that night. Waters had walked Alex through it moment by moment; he attacked Murdaugh's "fuzzy" memory of details, including Alex's last words to his wife and son; Waters mocked Alex's story about resting after an early supper, describing it as the quickest nap ever; Waters asked Alex if he meant what he told the jury — that he had tried to help police find the killers.

Alex: "Other than lying to them about going to the kennels, I was cooperative in every aspect of this investigation."

Waters: "Very cooperative except maybe about the most important fact of all, that you were at the murder scene with the victims just minutes before they died!"

Waters rattled off the names of almost 50 people starting with Maggie and Paul, and followed by Alex's family members, friends, law partners, clients and police who he had lied to, manipulated or deceived. "And now you want this jury to believe a story manufactured to fit the evidence that you brought forth after hearing a trial's worth of testimony?" Waters said.

The prosecutor was not through with Alex Murdaugh. He showed body-camera video of Alex talking to the first county deputy to arrive at the murder scene. With the bodies of his wife and son visible on that video, Alex lied when he said he did not see his wife and son for 45 minutes prior to leaving the Moselle house for Almeda. Indeed, Waters said, Alex had repeated this lie to authorities for the next 20 months. Waters said Alex had testified he did not trust SLED investigators, although he did have confidence in local authorities. Waters reminded everyone that Alex had testified he became paranoid about state agents when they interviewed him at the murder scene because he had pain pills that were in his pocket.

That's when Waters lowered the proverbial boom on Alex Murdaugh.

The prosecutor played a clip of the 911 call during which Alex lied about last seeing Maggie and Paul alive when they had an early supper together, and about being shocked soon after returning to Moselle from Almeda and finding his loved ones' bodies. Waters pointed out that Alex had lied when he told Colleton deputies he "trusted" as well as the 911 dispatcher that he had not been at the kennels earlier that evening with Maggie and Paul before the SLED crime team arrived from Columbia.

On the morning of March 1, 2023, the jurors were driven in a van to Moselle to see for themselves the crime scene, how close the kennels are to the main house, and both roads in and out of the property. The jurors returned around midday to the courthouse, and closing arguments soon followed. It had been 27 days of testimony since the trial began.

Waters spoke first, using powerful words and body language to recap the brutality of the murders:

— Paul was the first to die as he stood in the feed room. His killer held the shotgun, stepped in front of the door and pulled the trigger. The blast hit Paul on the right side of his chest and armpit. It spun Paul around to face his killer. Paul shuffled forward slightly before the second blast struck him in the head. His brain was blown from his cranium, he fell face first through the door, his body across the kennel's paved walkway.

— Maggie had heard the first shot and was "running toward her baby" when she saw her son being hit by the second blast.

— Moments later she was shot several times, killed at close range by her husband.

Waters said Alex had the motive, the means and the opportunity to murder them, and that he had made sure they were dead before calling 911 that night. But Alex did not know that Paul had used his cellphone to record the audio/video message that placed his father at the murder scene minutes before the shooting started. It took almost a year for investigators to unlock the video from Paul's phone, and for the prosecution to enter it into evidence. As the jury watched and listened to the recording, they saw and heard Paul's testimony from the grave.

"Why in the world would an innocent, reasonable husband and father lie about that, and lie so early?" Waters asked the jury.

Alex showed no emotion this time — no tears, no sniveling, no rocking back and forth as usual. He eyed Waters and he eyed each juror. Alex looked fierce, focused and analytical like the lawyer his father, grandfather and his great-grandfather had destined him to be. But at that moment almost everyone in the courtroom was convinced that Alex Murdaugh had committed South Carolina's crime of a century — a double-familicide in a crime saga that started more than a hundred years earlier when Randolph Murdaugh Sr. began practicing law in Hampton, S.C.

Waters summarized more than five weeks of testimony, the timeline of the murders, evidence and motives for the killings. He described what he called a perfect storm of financial woes and drug abuse bearing down on Alex in the withering summer of 2021. Soon after the murders, pressure on Alex from the boat accident had eased, and his colleagues seemed to rally around a grieving father and husband, Waters said. However the reprieve was short for the privileged man from a prominent family who had managed to avoid accountability almost his entire life. Alex Murdaugh was in fact a drug-addict living a lie, out of money and no longer able to beg, borrow, or steal it fast enough to save himself, the prosecutor said.

The state's case was built on a mountain of circumstantial evidence. It included testimony from more than 70 witnesses and the entry of approximately 400 pieces of evidence about missing family weapons, tell-tale cellphone data, precise GPS data found on Murdaugh's truck and his mad dash on the evening of the murders to Almeda and back, his raincoat with gunshot residue, and most importantly, Paul's last video that recorded Alex's voice in the background.

"The timeline puts him there. The use of his family weapons collaborates that, and his lies and guilty actions confirm it," Waters continued while stressing that Murdaugh was a part-time prosecutor who knew how criminal investigations worked, that he used two guns to make it appear there was more than one killer, and that he made multiple phone calls after the killings to manufacture his alibi.

The prosecutor described the "tangled web" of falsehoods that Murdaugh himself had admitted during his testimony. Waters said it began when Alex called 911 and included his changed story about where he was moments before his wife and son were killed. Waters reminded the jury that Murdaugh himself had testified that drug withdrawals "will make you do anything." Waters held up a file of photographs of Paul's and Maggie's bullet-ravaged bodies so graphic that Judge Newman had ordered them sealed from public view. "This is what he did. This is what he did right here," Waters said. "This defendant has fooled everyone ... He fooled everyone close to him ... He fooled them all. He fooled Maggie and Paul, and they paid for it with their lives. Don't let him fool you, too."

On the final day of the trial, Judge Newman announced the dismissal of a juror accused of discussing the case outside the courtroom. He politely thanked the woman and she was escorted out of the courtroom. She carried her purse, which contained a dozen farm-fresh eggs she said she had planned to share with other jurors that day.

Defense attorney James Griffin's closing argument cited a long list of what he described as fabrications by state police and prosecutors. He said SLED failed to properly preserve the crime scene or thoroughly investigate the killings. He questioned the authenticity of blood-spatter evidence, and said residue on the blue raincoat could have occurred before the murders. He criticized state investigators for focusing only on Murdaugh. He said they should have searched the Almeda property for murder weapons sooner than they did.

"We've shown conclusively that SLED failed miserably in investigating this case," he said, and described the state's case as "outlandish, irrational and insane." He said the evidence against his client was circumstantial then asked the jurors to use their common sense and the facts of the case, not theories or speculations, before rendering a verdict.

"You've heard weeks of testimony about Alex Murdaugh's financial condition, his addiction, and his lies, but what you haven't heard is a satisfactory answer to the question, Why would he do it?" Griffin said, adding, "There are two words justice demands in this case, and those words are 'not guilty'. On behalf of Maggie and my friend Paul, don't compound a family tragedy with another one."

The prosecution's final rebuttal was presented by state assistant attorney general John Meadors, of Columbia, a gifted Southern lawyer who reminded observers of actor Andy Griffin's character in the classic "Matlock" television series. Meadors talked about common sense, what's real and what's not, and the importance of making right choices. He reminded the jury of Murdaugh's reactions when faced with contradictory evidence. He said

Murdaugh lied for 627 days about when he left Moselle before taking the stand and changing his alibi. "I think he did it to protect the person he loved the most — Alex," Meadors said, adding that Murdaugh did not go to Almeda that evening to see his ailing mother; he went to Almeda to hide the murder weapons. "He wasn't going there because he loved his momma; he was going there because he loved Alex," Meadors said. "Alex loved himself more than Paul and Maggie."

Meadors recapped the testimony of **Blanca Turrubiate-Simpson**, the housekeeper, and Shelley Smith, the caretaker — both of whom he described as "real people." Meadors then said Paul testified to the truth through the final video he recorded in his life. "And isn't it something that your best witness is a dog? … Thank God for Bubba!"

The initial jury had four white men and eight women, two of them African Americans — all from rural Colleton County. Five jurors were replaced by alternates. Some were excused for medical emergencies, others for testing positive for covid exposure, and one accused of improper contact with a member of the public. Early in the trial the cramped old courthouse in a small Southern town was evacuated following a bomb threat, followed by a whirlwind of testimony about shotguns, AR-15-style semi-automatic rifles, wild-hog hunting and a chicken-killing dog named Bubba, which became a hero of sorts for the prosecution. The trial was covered daily by local, regional, national and international newspapers, major television networks and radio stations. It also had a huge, cult-like following on social media.

The fate of Alex Murdaugh and what remained of his family legacy would be decided by a jury of seven white men and five women, two of them black. Only one alternate remained in the event that something else went wrong.

28

The Monster You've Become

"Oh, monsters are scared," said Lettie. "That's why they're monsters."
— Neil Gaiman, author, *The Ocean at the End of the Lane*

WALTERBORO, March 2, 2023 —

The jury left the courtroom to begin deliberations, and members of the media did not venture far from the courthouse. No one knew how long it would take to get a verdict. Prosecutors had no murder weapons, no eye-witnesses and no absolute proof Murdaugh killed his wife and son. However, circumstantial evidence, especially Paul's video and technical data from Alex's vehicle, was powerful. Would it be enough to convict Alex Murdaugh?

The answer came sooner than most observers thought. The sun had set and the lights powered up in the media city enveloping the courthouse, where word got out Judge Newman had instructed the bailiff to bring back in the jury. The courtroom quickly filled, and just after 7 p.m. the judge declared the court was again in session. The jury had deliberated only three hours.

Earlier that day Alex Murdaugh appeared confident, almost smug. He did not now. Colleton County Clerk of Court Rebecca Hill slowly and dramatically read out each of the four indictments. Alex stared straight ahead until a verdict of "guilty" was issued on the first count. He stiffened up. As the same verdict was rendered on each of the three remaining counts, he turned and rocked a little. Alex's brothers were not in the courtroom. His sister and surviving son showed little emotion: Lynn wiped her eyes; Buster's face turned bright red.

Alex's attorneys asked Judge Newman to declare a mistrial, which was denied. They next asked him to set aside the verdict. "We have been here 28 days," the judge said. "The evidence of guilt is overwhelming, and I deny the motion." He announced he would render the sentence at 9:30 the following morning.

As a court security officer cuffed Murdaugh to lead him away, Alex turned his head toward his son, nodded and mouthed some unintelligible words. Buster looked down briefly then away as his father was escorted out of the courtroom. Before excusing the jurors, Judge Newman thanked them for their service and said, "It's not often you are called upon to sit in judgement of your fellow man, and you responded. The circumstantial evidence, the direct evidence, all pointed to only one conclusion, and that is what you all reached."

As the courtroom cleared, prosecutors and SLED agents smiled and hugged in celebration. Some were teary-eyed. The almost two-year investigation and month-long trial were over, and they had gotten their man. Journalists, curious lawyers and other observers gathered in small groups outside and talked quietly among themselves. Not long afterward S.C. Attorney General Alan Wilson and his team gathered for a press conference in front of the courthouse. A celebratory buzz arose as television lights illuminated the square and members of the media elbowed for positions to cover the press conference.

Prosecutor Creighton Waters stepped to the microphones, said it been a tough, demanding trial and thanked the jurors for their service. "This was a team effort and amazing work ... on a complex case. It doesn't matter how much money someone has, if you do wrong, break the law and murder, justice will be done in South Carolina."

Attorney General Wilson also spoke: "Our criminal justice system gave a voice to Maggie and Paul Murdaugh ... We can't bring them back, but we did bring them justice. Today's verdict proves that no one, no matter who they are in society, is above the law." He thanked the local, state and federal agencies involved, then said: "When you go home tonight, hug your loved ones, hug your spouse, hug your children. You can't take them for granted."

Throughout the trial Alex wore a dress shirt and sports coat as the eyes of the jurors and the millions of other people around the world were upon him. But the next morning they saw him shuffle into the courtroom wearing a baggy Colleton County jail jumpsuit and looking like the condemned man he was. The room was full of reporters and spectators. Also there were numerous state and local officers who had been maligned by the defense during the trial. Phillip Beach, father of Mallory Beach who died on the doomed boat ride, was there. Although the jurors were not required to be in attendance, all but one were there too.

Waters told Judge Newman that none of the victims' family members chose to make statements and no one wanted to speak on Alex's behalf. Waters described Paul as a loving, loyal friend and he said Maggie was a "girl's girl" who doted on her sons. He said neither victim knew what their killer had become. But in time the real Alex Murdaugh was exposed. "The depravity, the callousness, the selfishness of these crimes are stunning," the prosecutor said, then pointed to Murdaugh. "Your honor, a man like that, a man like this man, should never be allowed to be among free, law-abiding citizens again."

Judge Newman soon responded: "For the murder of your son, Paul, who I am sure you loved very much, I sentence you to prison for the rest of your natural life …" Then he issued the same sentence to Alex for killing his wife.

The prosecutors had announced before the start of the trial that it would not be a death penalty case — that the maximum sentence would be life in prison for Alex Murdaugh, presumably because the evidence was all circumstantial. After Newman announced the life sentences for Alex, the judge said his crimes certainly qualified for the death penalty. Newman noted that scores of people prosecuted by members of the Murdaugh dynasty "got the death penalty for far less." Judge Newman described the case against Alex Murdaugh as among the most troubling he had ever seen. He looked at Alex and said, "It was especially heartbreaking to see you go in the media from a grieving father who lost a wife and son to being the person convicted of killing them … a lawyer, a person from a respected family who has controlled justice in this community for over a century."

Murdaugh responded: "As I tell you again, I respect this court. But I am innocent. I would never under any circumstances hurt my wife, Maggie, and I would never under any circumstances hurt my son Paul-Paul."

Judge Newman: "It might not have been you … It might have been the monster you become when you take 15, 20, 30, 40, 50, 60 opioid pills." Newman also said he was convinced that regardless of who Alex might become, "You will see Paul and Maggie at night when you are attempting to go to sleep. I'm sure they come and visit you, I'm sure."

Murdaugh: "All day and every night."

Newman: "I'm sure."

The judge said he would soon schedule hearings for the remainder of scores of state cases alleging Alex had also committed financial frauds and drug-related crimes, then banged his gavel. Murdaugh — shackled, defeated, his head hanging low — turned to his right and shuffled out of the courtroom.

Alex was convicted of the unthinkable for a member of his clan — he had shed Murdaugh blood and betrayed the family name that had given him everything. But despite the evidence and the conviction, many people, including his own surviving son, doubt he was guilty of pulling the triggers. Murmurs and rumors darted in the shadows. Alex's attorneys caught wind of a foul rumor about an attempt to influence the jury by an officer of the court. Would it be enough to grant Alex a re-trial?

29
MONSTER REBORN

The victors stood tall as they emerged from the Walterboro courthouse after Alex was escorted out through a side door. One observer later cross-stitched effigies of feisty lead prosecutor Creighton Waters and others who had brought the killer to justice — including Bubba, the hunting dog that had introduced the dead chicken as a critical piece of evidence. Entrepreneurs would also sell T-shirts and hats on which were quoted the judge's memorable, Southern-drawled catchphrase, "Brang the Jury!"

Crime scene investigator Dr. Kenny Kinsey of Orangeburg was mobbed by reporters and autograph-seekers. Jurors sent word that they wanted to meet with Kinsey, and thank him. "For me, it was all about getting justice for the victims," he told reporters as he stood on the courthouse lawn.

Juror Craig Moyer told ABC News that when deliberations began, the jury took a straw poll that showed nine guilty votes, but it didn't take long to convince the other three. Most of the jurors agreed that the key evidence was Paul's video, which had been locked on his cellphone for a year while Alex repeatedly lied about where he was five minutes before the shooting started. They said they were offended when Alex pretended to cry and attempted to manipulate the jury while on the stand.

"A good liar. But not good enough," Moyer said.

Four generations of Murdaugh men had steadfastly protected their families and fortunes during times of trouble. But Alex committed the unthinkable — he murdered his wife and son in a failed attempt to save himself. No longer was he an esteemed son of the proud Murdaugh clan, a descendant of a Confederate hero, a respected member of his community. He was utterly shamed: S.C. Department of Corrections Inmate Number 00390394. His prison mugshot is haunting, his eyes and face diabolical, calculating. After a brief evaluation period, he was placed under protective custody at an undisclosed maximum security state prison to begin two consecutive life sentences without the possibility of parole. "That first life sentence is going to be hard, but that second one ought to be pretty easy," joked one lawyer who asked to remain anonymous.

Within days, Murdaugh's attorneys filed a notice of appeal, vowing to fight his conviction all the way to the Supreme Court. But it was unclear how Alex would pay his lawyers. His assets were seized, his estates sold, his furniture and belongings auctioned off to the highest bidder. And he still faced more than a hundred federal and state financial as well as drug charges. On May 23 a federal grand jury in U.S. District Court in Charleston returned a 28-page, 22-count indictment against Murdaugh for wire fraud, bank fraud, conspiracy to commit wire fraud and bank fraud, and money laundering. Accomplice Cory Fleming, a Beaufort lawyer, was also charged but made a plea agreement in exchange for his cooperation against Murdaugh.

By March 12, nine days after his arrival at the Kirkland Correction Institution for evaluation, Inmate Number 00390394 was receiving mail from female admirers — some expressing love, some offering to send photos of themselves. "I think I love you," wrote someone who identified as Nicollette K. "I think about you all day every day. I swear on my life I'll never say a single word to anyone important or not important. I genuinely care for you." The same day, another note arrived: "I am just a small town girl from Missouri. I am here if you want to talk. Or vent. XXLacie."

Such dispatches from people purporting to be desperate damsels made a big splash on Columbia's *FITS News,* as did a message from the producers of the hit Netflix documentary, "Murdaugh Murders: A Southern Scandal," which aired during the trial: "We feel at this point it's very important to have your voice in the (remainder) of our series," producer Mike Gasparro wrote. "Our first three episodes (were) viewed by 40 million households and also 75 million hours (were) watched in just ten days. Those numbers will continue to rise. We believe you can have the largest platform on TV if you are willing to speak to us."

Fox Nation, a cable news special channel, produced a three-part documentary featuring a prison interview with Alex and another with his surviving son Buster Murdaugh. The title of the Fox News special is the same as the main title of this book.

30

EXHUMATION

SATURDAY, APRIL 1, 2023 —

As markers and yellow lines flashed by, the State Law Enforcement Division caravan cruised south down Interstate 95 on a morbid mission. State police and privately hired examiners were escorting the unearthed remains of Stephen Smith to an undisclosed forensic autopsy lab in Florida. Eight years after Smith's death, and in the wake of the Murdaugh murder trial, SLED officially classified the case as a homicide.

Sandy Smith had mourned her slain son since 2015, and now she had a new lawyer: Eric Bland, who won the Satterfield case — and she could afford it thanks to proceeds from internet-driven GoFundMe campaigns to exhume her son's body for an independent autopsy. They hired top forensic pathologists along with crime-scene expert Dr. Kenny Kinsey, who had done an exceptional job as a prosecution witness in the Murdaugh trial. Meanwhile, SLED pledged full support in a new probe for answers about who or what killed Stephen Smith.

Young Smith had been pursuing a career in nursing at Orangeburg-Calhoun Technical College when he died. His body was found across the centerline of paved rural road, and he had obviously been hit in the head. Officially, Smith was listed as the victim of a hit-and-run driver. However, his mother and others doubted that narrative, especially in light of rumors that sons of a well-to-do family were involved. They were convinced Stephen was the victim of a hate crime. The media frenzy surrounding the Alex Murdaugh double-murder conviction was enough to revive even the coldest of cases.

In the fall of 2021, the push to revive the case of Stephen Smith, who was buried in Gooding Cemetery near Hampton, got a significant boost. The #StandingForStephen effort, deeply rooted in the South Carolina LGBTQ community, began raising money for the family's search for answers. By July 2022 the movement's GoFundMe account had raised more than $40,000 to pay for Stephen's gravestone as well as a marker for his father, who died three months after his son's death, and to help cover Mrs. Smith's legal expenses.

Soon after Alex's conviction, a second fundraiser called #justiceforstephensmith was launched with proceeds designated to cover an independent investigation. By Sept. 1, 2023, the second fund-raising effort received $130,125 in donations from around the world. Sandy Smith's initial attorney, Mike Hemlepp Jr., described Stephen as a fallen warrior for LGBTQ youth. "Imagine what kind of doctor he could have been for gay kids, but he was not because someone bashed his head in. … The time for being sad is over. I'm no longer sad. I'm mad, and I want more. It's time to get angry. It's time to get answers. It's time to get solutions. We don't honor Stephen by being sad. The way to honor Stephen is to get mad."

Stephen's remains were re-examined, returned to Hampton and reburied. The results have yet to be announced, and apparently state lawmen continue to investigate the circumstances surrounding his death. Meanwhile, on March 20, 2023, Alex Murdaugh's oldest son, Buster, issued a public statement:

"I have tried my best to ignore the vicious rumors about my involvement in Stephen Smith's tragic death that continue to be published in the media as I grieve over the brutal murders of my mother and brother. I love them so much and miss them terribly. I haven't spoken up until now because I want to live in private while I cope with their deaths and my father's incarceration.

"Before, during and since my father's trial, I have been targeted and harassed by the media and followers of this story. This has gone on far too long. These baseless rumors of my involvement with Stephen and his death are false. I unequivocally deny any involvement in his death, and my heart goes out to the Smith family. I am requesting that the media immediately stop publishing these defamatory comments and rumors about me."

Meanwhile, the family of the late-Gloria Satterfield decided to form a foundation in her honor and dedicated to helping needy families annually during the Christmas holidays. Mrs. Satterfield was the housekeeper at Molselle who fell down the front steps of the house, hit her head, and was hospitalized for weeks before she passed away. Family members described her as a quiet, down-to-earth woman who worked hard and especially enjoyed family gatherings during the Christmas holidays. It took years before her sons actually collected a multimillion-dollar insurance settlement on a policy that Alex Murdaugh had to cover accidents at Moselle.

The establishment of Gloria's Gift Foundation in the summer of 2022 provides money to pay for gifts and meals during the holidays to needy families in Hampton County.

On June 16, 2022, the Palmetto Theater on Lee Avenue was filled with dignitaries, members of the Satterfield family, and media members for a press conference called by the Bland and Richter law firm, which represented Mrs. Satterfield's estate. It was no ordinary presser: *Hampton County Guardian* Editor Michael DeWitt was not there to ask questions. He had agreed to say a few words in praise of the Hampton County community:

"I hope you all realize the full magnitude of the moment we are in. Today is not just a press conference. This is not just some charity. We are at a turning point in a story that will become South Carolina history. As of today, this is no longer Alex Murdaugh's story of crime and corruption ... As of today, this is Gloria Satterfield's story and this is Mallory Beach's story. This is Act Two ... it's about the victims and justice. With this announcement of Gloria's gift to the community, these victims have transformed an act of evil into something wonderful. These victims are getting the final say, the last word. And that last word is love..."

Gloria's sister Ginger Harriott Hadwin also spoke:
"After having fought the good fight for justice, we chose to make sure that Gloria's lasting legacy will not be that of a victim, but will be as a champion for love and charity. She was humble, she was a Southern lady filled with gratitude and grace... She was so much more than just a housekeeper. She had a full, pure heart of kindness and love for everyone she met."

Family attorney Eric Bland added:
"Today is about redefining Gloria's legacy. The family got sick and tired of hearing that she was just a housekeeper, that she was 'Murdaugh's housekeeper.' She was far more than a housekeeper. She was someone who loved, lived, laughed."

Gloria's family presented a check for $55,000 to establish the Gloria's Gifts charity fund. It was followed by an additional $20,000 check from the law firm. The investment goal was to provide annually up to $500 in gifts for at least 20 deserving Hampton County families the first year and become an on-going example of victory of good over evil. Gloria's Gift launched during the Christmas of 2022, providing 32 area children with Christmas gifts and clothing, and by September 2023 work began to serve more local people in need the following year.

It should be noted that not only humans have been blessed by others in the on-going Murdaugh story. Mallory Beach, who died in the boating accident in Beaufort, loved animals, especially puppies. She rescued them, fostered them, snuggled with them, and even buckled them up in her car for drives around the countryside. "She always had an animal with her or would pick up strays and bring them home," her mother, Renee, said.

Mallory's death launched multiple criminal investigations and lawsuits involving Alex Murdaugh. A nonprofit foundation, Mal's Palz, was established in her memory to raise money to improve and expand the Hampton County animal shelter and eventually build a new facility. The foundation has thus far raised more than $52,000.

EPILOGUE

"Crime is a sprinter; justice is built for the long run."
— **Attorney Ronnie Richter, Greenville, S.C.**

If Alex Murdaugh hoped to hide his secrets in the foggy bottoms of the 14th Judicial Circuit, his optimism has surely vanished. His schemes first arose into the light of truth when young Mallory Beach's body was recovered in the marsh on a sad winter day in 2019. They illuminated the night in the spring of 2021 as emergency vehicles screamed down back roads of Colleton County in route to the Murdaugh hunting estate where the bodies of Maggie and son Paul Murdaugh were awash in blood. And it's no secret now that Alex botched his staged suicide alongside Old Salkehatchie Road on the 2021 Labor Day weekend.

Alex was convicted in 2023 of murdering his wife and son, and sentenced to two consecutive life terms without parole. However, questions still linger and a final resolution of his crimes has yet to come. Murdaugh murder mania swept the English-speaking world, and a new wave of Netflix and other such "entertainment" is sure to come.

For six weeks during Alex's double-murder trial, his son, Richard Alexander "Buster" Murdaugh Jr., sat watching and listening as a mountain of evidence and testimony was pitched, proffered and probed on how his father killed Maggie and Paul with weapons designed to dispatch wild hogs and whitetail deer. He sat stone-faced as prosecutors documented his father's race to the house in Almeda and back in a failed attempt to establish his alibi.

On Aug. 31, 2023, Alex's only surviving son shared what promised to be his innermost thoughts with Fox News' Martha MacCallum in a special three-part television documentary. Buster said his father did not get a fair and impartial murder trial, and criticized the work of law enforcement officers, the judge and the jury. He said Alex was incapable of killing his beloved wife and youngest son. In addition, Buster denied any involvement in young

Stephen Smith's mysterious death as well as any romantic involvement with his openly gay high school classmate. Buster said he was at his family's Edisto beach house the night Smith's body was found in the middle of a paved road not far from Moselle.

However, Buster confirmed that his father was psychopathic, a liar, a thief and a manipulator. He also said he wanted to revive the Murdaugh family's good name. Buster, who plans to be readmitted to law school and earn a degree, said he did not want to be portrayed as another sad character in the shocking fall of the house of Murdaugh.

"It feels like anybody that maintains the last name Murdaugh now has a horrible stain on their integrity because there's obviously a perception," he told Fox Nation. "People think like, oh, the apple doesn't fall very far from the tree."

The Murdaugh dynasty along with the "good old boy" system that fostered it will not be forgotten. Alex Murdaugh was at the eye of a capacious storm of callous conspiracy and violent crime. His family is legendary, and fallout from his twisted conceit continues to rain down on the S.C. Lowcountry both inside courtrooms and out. Will anything good come from it? Will judicial reform and the public's insistence on honest leadership be left in the wake? It took four years of bitter wrangling before civil justice was served for the family of Mallory Beach. Must resolution take so long and at such a heavy toll?

It wasn't until July 2023 that insurance companies representing the Parker's Kitchen convenience store at Okatie agreed to pay $18 million because a clerk misread a driver's license and sold beer and hard seltzer to underaged Paul Murdaugh prior to the deadly boat crash. Of that total, $15 million went to the Beach family, and approximately $130,000 from legal fees were donated in Mallory's honor to Mal's Palz animal foundation.

Most civil settlements are confidential, but Renee Beach's attorney said his client insisted this one be made public as a reminder to parents and everyone else that enabling underage drinking is not only dangerous but can also be extremely expensive. Meanwhile, Mrs. Beach's parallel lawsuit against Parker's for alleged harassment and intimidation during the course of the wrongful-death case has yet to be resolved.

Alex Murdaugh himself has neither paid the Beach family anything nor acknowledged any responsibility for Mallory's death. All of Alex's known assets have been seized by authorities while the remainder of civil and federal lawsuits against him are pending.

The following is a brief roundup of what has happened after Alex Murdaugh was deemed guilty of killing his wife and son:

— Former Palmetto State Bank CEO Russell Laffitte was convicted in federal court and sentenced to 84 months in federal prison for his role in helping Alex Murdaugh defraud clients. Laffitte got seven years in federal prison and was ordered to pay $3.5 million in restitution to victims or their suvivors. He also faces similar conspiracy and fraud charges on the state level. Like Murdaugh, Laffitte is a Hampton County native and scion of a well-known S.C. banking family.

"This sentencing says that you can't run from justice, no matter how powerful of a family you come from or how powerful of a person you are in our state," one of the victim's attorneys, Eric Bland, said. "The rule of law will hunt you down and get you, and you will pay the same penalty as everyone else."

— Alex Murdaugh's college roommate and Paul's godfather Cory Fleming was also indicted in both federal and state courts. Fleming, 54, who was a Beaufort lawyer, pleaded guilty to federal charges and agreed to cooperate with Murdaugh investigators. Fleming was sentenced to three years and eight months in federal custody, followed by three years of court-ordered supervision and probation, as well as paying $102,222 in restitution and a $20,000 fine. He reported to federal authorities in early August 2023 and has begun serving his sentence. A week later he pleaded guilty to all S.C. charges against him before Judge Newman, who has adjudicated all Murdaugh-related state criminal cases to date. Fleming offered to work with authorities in the hope of getting a reduced sentence.

The Beaufort County Courthouse was packed in September with Fleming's family and friends who lauded his character and requested mercy. Fleming maintained that he was recruited and duped by his longtime friend Alex Murdaugh. Fleming, wearing a blue and gray stripe prison jumpsuit, wept as he pleaded for leniency. However, Judge Newman sentenced him to more than ten years in state prison, to be served consecutively with his federal 45-month sentence. If he behaves in prison, Fleming might get out after serving almost 14 years.

That same day, Alex was taken from his prison cell to Beaufort for a separate hearing. Alex was dressed in an orange S.C. Detention Center jumpsuit and shackled as he was led into the courtroom by a corrections officer. It was the same room where his late-son Paul was arraigned four years earlier for boating under the influence of alcohol when Mallory Beach died. Over the objections of Murdaugh's attorneys, Judge Newman set the first trial date for Alex's financial crimes for Nov. 27, 2023 in Beaufort County General Sessions Court.

— On Aug. 17, 2023, Jerry K. Rivers, 40, of Walterboro, pleaded guilty to fraud, money laundering, drug charges and other crimes before Judge Newman. According to state prosecutors, Rivers was the primary provider of Roxicodone and Oxycodone pills to Curtis Edward Smith, and thus to Alex Murdaugh. During his plea hearing, Rivers maintained that he had never met with Alex and did not know him personally.

— A trial date was scheduled for Dec. 18, 2023 in Colleton County for Spencer Roberts, an alleged Alex Murdaugh associate involved in drug dealing and an illegal gambling operation in the S.C. Lowcountry.

— Curtis Edward "Cousin Eddie" Smith, the alleged accomplice in Alex's botched suicide attempt on Old Salkehatchie Road, cooperated with Murdaugh investigators and was allowed to remain at his Walterboro home on bond as he dealt with health problems.

— While Alex is lodged in an undisclosed state prison, it has been widely reported that he is expected to serve out his life sentences in the S.C. correctional facility in McCormick, S.C. It was also reported that, like other inmates, he had access to a state telephone and a state-issued computer tablet on which his outside correspondence was recorded. A number of people purporting to be women have contacted him, and somehow photos of Alex, shirtless, inside a jail cell have been posted on the Internet. On Aug. 30, 2023, the S.C. Department of Corrections revoked his telephone and tablet privileges for participating in the Fox interview, cutting him off from the outside world — at least temporarily.

— Alex Murdaugh participated in a jail-cell telephone interview that was used in the Fox Nation television series that also featured conversations with his surviving son Buster. The interview was apparently done without the knowledge of state Department of Corrections officials. Alex's interview was allegedly recorded by one of his defense lawyers under the guise of client-attorney privilege. During the documentary, Alex insisted that he did not murder his wife and youngest son, and said he would hold his head up high on his personal "journey," which will include his court appeals.

— On March 6, 2023, the Monday after the guilty verdict and sentencing, Colleton County Clerk of Court Rebecca Hill and her staff set about re-turning the county courthouse to normalcy. Hill, a descendant of Colleton bootleggers once betrayed by the Murdaugh clan and others, climbed a ladder and rehung the oil portrait of former solicitor Randolph "Buster" Murdaugh Jr., to look down on court proceedings. Tourists from up and down Interstate 95 have been stopping in Walterboro to gawk at the now-famous courthouse and hear behind-the-scenes tales of the trial. With the replacement of the painting, they can also view a former face of local justice.

— Most folks were surprised that, not long after Murdaugh was found guilty of killing his wife and son, Colleton County Clerk of Court Rebecca Hill pub-lished a memoir titled *Behind the Doors of Justice: The Murdaugh Murders*. It included her experiences with the Murdaugh family, her moonshine-making ancestors, and her role as clerk during the trial. After reading the book, Alex's attorneys claimed that Hill had tampered with the jurors by interacting too closely with them before and during deliberations. They have requested a new double-murder trial for Alex Murdaugh.

On Nov. 21, SLED charged Colleton County Clerk of Court Becky Hill's son, Jeffrey Colton Hill, 34, with wiretapping of a court official, and new controversies begin.

Roll Call of Pain, Suffering

The life sentences for the deaths of Maggie and Paul Murdaugh were merely two small drops of justice in an empty well of pain, betrayal, and loss. In addition to murder charges, Richard Alexander Murdaugh was indicted in connection with a decade-long, multi-county, multiple-victim financial crime spree in which he allegedly stole more than $8.7 million. According to the S.C. State Grand Jury charges, Murdaugh stole from family, friends, partners, and clients who trusted him. He allegedly stole from the living, from the injured and the grieving, and even the dead.

The stolen funds represented money these people desperately needed for medical expenses, burial expenses, and normal living expenses after experiencing something traumatic in their lives. Murdaugh didn't just steal money from these victims, he robbed them of their trust, their security, their hope, their chance for a better tomorrow.

Below is a list of all known financial victims, according to attorneys and state indictments. This list may be incomplete, as this is a complex case, and there may be other victims not yet named by law enforcement, or who haven't come forward.

Allendale County
Arthur Badger
Estate of Donna Badger
Deon Martin

Colleton County
Manuel Santis-Cristiani
Christopher Anderson
Estate of Sandra Taylor

Orangeburg County
Thomas L. Moore

Beaufort County
Jordan Jinks
Estate of Blondell Gary

Hampton County
Gloria Satterfield
Tony Satterfield, Brian Harriot, and the Estate of Gloria Satterfield
Sandra Manning
Johnny Bush
Jamian Risher
Randy Drawdy
Hakeem Pinckney
Estate of Hakeem Pinckney
Natasha Thomas
Alaynia Spohn
Hannah Plyler

Corporate victims include insurance companies and partners of the old PMPED law firm, which was changed to the Parker Law Group.

The Murdaugh Men

Josiah Putnam Murdaugh II (1840-1912)

Randolph Murdaugh Sr. (Feb. 28, 1887 – July 19, 1940)

Randolph "Buster" Murdaugh Jr. (Jan. 9, 1915 – Feb. 5, 1998)

Randolph "Handsome" Murdaugh III (Oct. 25, 1939 – June 10, 2021)

Richard Alexander Murdaugh (May 27, 1968 –)

Richard Alexander "Buster" Murdaugh Jr. (1996 –)

Paul Terry Murdaugh (1999 – June 7, 2018)

A Murdaugh Dynasty Timeline

April 9, 1865 – General Robert E. Lee surrenders to General Grant. J.P. Murdaugh II is reportedly there, a private in the Confederate Army.

Feb. 28, 1887 – Randolph Murdaugh Sr. is born, one of several children of J.P. Murdaugh II.

Summer 1910 – Randolph Murdaugh Sr. graduates from law school and founds the Murdaugh law firm, which would add partners and later become PMPED.

Aug. 17, 1912 – J.P. Murdaugh II dies, leaving behind wealth, land, and several children, including Randolph Murdaugh Sr.

Jan. 9, 1915 – Randolph "Buster" Murdaugh Jr. is born, one of two sons of Randolph Sr.

Sept. 15, 1918 – Buster Murdaugh's mother, Etta Harvey Murdaugh, dies, drawing Buster closer to his lawyer father, who remarries twice.

Summer 1938 – Buster Murdaugh begins practicing law, joining his father at the Murdaugh law firm and serving as assistant solicitor.

July 1939 – The Hampton County Watermelon Festival is founded. Over the years, both Randolph Murdaugh Jr. and Randolph III would be honored as Grand Marshals.

July 19, 1940 – Randolph Murdaugh Sr. is killed by a train in Hampton County. The S.C. Governor appoints his son, Randolph "Buster" Murdaugh Jr., as interim solicitor to fill the unexpired term. Buster is later elected in his own right to serve more than four decades at the post.

Oct. 1, 1940 – Randolph "Buster" Murdaugh Jr. files a wrongful-death suit against the train company following the crash that killed his father.

September 1941 – The wrongful-death suit is settled for an undisclosed amount of money, launching the Murdaugh legacy of profiting from personal-injury lawsuits filed against railroad companies and others.

June 5, 1956 – After more than a decade of allegations and controversies, Buster Murdaugh is indicted on federal conspiracy charges related to moonshine production and sales in a case the media called "The Great Colleton County Whiskey Conspiracy."

Oct. 1, 1956 – The Great Colleton County Whiskey Conspiracy ends after a lengthy federal trial in Charleston. Buster Murdaugh and two other defendants are acquitted, while more than a score of others are convicted and sent to federal prison.

Nov. 6, 1956 – 14th Judicial Solicitor Buster Murdaugh is swept back into office by a sizable majority of voters in all five counties of the circuit, and on Nov. 19 the governor officially returns him to his post.

Summer 1964 – Randolph Murdaugh III graduates from law school, begins serving "unofficially" as Buster's assistant solicitor, and in 1969 his assignment was made official. It was a post Randolph III would hold until 1986, when he replaced his retiring father as solicitor.

May 27, 1968 – Richard "Alex" Murdaugh is born, one of four children of Randolph Murdaugh III and Elizabeth "Libby" Murdaugh.

Jan. 1, 1977 – A new S.C. law takes effect mandating that the office of solicitor be a full-time position and prohibiting prosecutors from private civil practice on the side, which impacted the Murdaughs with their personal injury law firm. Buster Murdaugh resigns from private practice.

Dec. 31, 1986 – Buster Murdaugh retires after 46 years as solicitor. Randolph III is appointed to replace him and then is elected in his own right in 1987.

Aug. 14, 1993 – Richard "Alex" Murdaugh marries Margaret "Maggie" Kennedy Branstetter. Alex and Maggie's first child, Richard Alexander "Buster" Murdaugh Jr., is born in 1996, and Paul Terry Murdaugh comes three years later.

Summer 1994 – Alex Murdaugh earns his law degree and not long afterward joins the family law firm and his father in the solicitor's office.

Feb. 5, 1998 – Randolph "Buster" Murdaugh Jr. dies.

Dec. 31, 2005 – Randolph Murdaugh III retires as solicitor after serving almost 20 years. The end of his term marked 85-plus years that the Randolph Murdaugh trilogy held the office of 14th Circuit Solicitor.

July 8, 2015 – The body of Stephen Smith is found lying on a rural Hampton County road. Rumors fly around town and are included in police reports mentioning a possible Murdaugh connection, which was not officially proven.

Feb. 2, 2018 – Murdaugh household employee Gloria Satterfield suffers a reported fall at Moselle, the Colleton County home of Alex and Maggie Murdaugh, and dies roughly three weeks later, setting off a chain of events that resulted in criminal charges and civil suits years later for Alex Murdaugh.

Sept. 20, 2018 – Randolph Murdaugh III is honored in a ceremony at the Hampton County Courthouse for receiving the Order of the Palmetto.

Feb. 24, 2019 – Paul Murdaugh and friends are involved in a boat crash in Archers Creek, Beaufort County, leaving Mallory Beach dead. This brought more negative attention and legal trouble to Alex Murdaugh and his family.

March 3, 2019 – Mallory Beach's body is found near a Broad River public boat landing, and hundreds turn out to mourn her in Hampton County.

March 20, 2019 – Renee Beach files the first version of her wrongful death suit in Beaufort County for the death of her daughter, Mallory, naming multiple parties, and ultimately the Murdaughs. On March 29, Mrs. Beach files an amended lawsuit in Hampton County and names Randolph Murdaugh III, Alex Murdaugh, his son, Buster, and a Murdaugh family trust.

April 18, 2019 – Paul Murdaugh is indicted on three counts of felony boating under the influence in a direct indictment from a Beaufort County grand jury. He was arraigned on the charges and released on bond May 6.

June 7, 2021 – PMPED Chief Financial Officer Jeannie Seckinger confronts Alex Murdaugh about missing legal fees.

June 7, 2021 – Paul and Maggie Murdaugh are found dead, shot multiple times in brutal fashion, at their Colleton County home, Moselle. Alex Murdaugh claims that he found the bodies, then called 911.

June 8, 2021 – SLED conducts its first interview with Alex in the early morning hours after the killings. They would interview him again on June 10, and then on Aug. 11, before officially ruling him a suspect.

Sept. 3, 2021 – PMPED partners meet with Alex Murdaugh over missing and allegedly stolen money, forcing him to resign and threatening to involve law enforcement.

Sept. 4, 2021 – Bizarre roadside shooting incident in which Alex Murduagh is injured.

Sept. 16, 2021 – The first criminal charges are levied against Alex Murdaugh. He turns himself in to authorities and is booked at the Hampton County Detention Center.

Nov. 19, 2021 – Alex Murdaugh gets the first of several indictments by S.C. State Grand Jury.

Jan. 4, 2022 – PMPED senior partners announce that they had dropped the Murdaugh name completely and would operate a new firm under the name Parker Law Group.

June 16, 2022 – The Gloria's Gift Foundation is established as a Christmas charity in Gloria Satterfield's memory.

July 2022 – The #StandingForStephen movement gains traction in support of the late Stephen Smith's family and young gay teens everywhere.

July 12, 2022 – Suspended attorney Alex Murdaugh is officially disbarred by the S.C. Supreme Court.

July 14, 2022 – Alex Murdaugh is indicted in the murders of his wife, Maggie, and son, Paul.

Jan. 23, 2023 – Alex Murdaugh's double-murder trial begins in Walterboro, S.C., with jury selection.

Jan. 25, 2023 – The Colleton County jury is sworn in, and opening statements begin in Alex Murdaugh's murder trial.

Feb. 1, 2023 – Alex Murdaugh's alibi is shredded during the trial by the introduction of a video placing him at the murder scene minutes before the killings.

Feb. 17, 2023 – The State rests its case against Alex Murdaugh, and the defense begins.

Feb. 23, 2023 – Alex Murdaugh takes the stand in his own defense. He testifies for more than ten hours in two days.

March 1, 2023 – The jury visits the crime scene — the kennels at Moselle — and then closing arguments begin.

March 2, 2023 – Alex Murdaugh is convicted by a Colleton County jury on four felony counts and found guilty of murdering both his wife and son.

March 3, 2023 – Judge Clifton Newman sentences Alex Murdaugh to two consecutive life terms in the state prison system.

April 1, 2023 – Driven by the publicity surrounding the Murdaugh murders trial, the cold case involving Stephen Smith's homicide re-ignites, and Smith's remains are exhumed for an independent autopsy. A new state investigation begins.

Bibliography

I n writing this work of nonfiction, the author relied heavily on his own
news gathering and reporting over the past two decades, personal interviews and conversations with members of the Murdaugh family and their
associates, and the following sources:

"125 Years, 1879-2004: Hampton County's History as Recorded on the Pages of *The Hampton County Guardian*." The Hampton County Guardian 125th Anniversary Edition, September 30, 2004.

Beaufort County Court of Common Pleas public records.

DeWitt Jr., Michael. *Images of America* – Hampton County. Arcadia Publishing, 2015.

Dickey, Gary C. "A Heritage in the Law: Randolph Murdaugh Jr. '38." *Carolina Lawyer: the University of South Carolina School of Law*; Volume IX, 1989. Pages 5 – 7.

Hampton County Court of Common Pleas public records.

Hampton County Court of General Sessions public records.

Hampton County Historical Society. *From the Salkehatchie to the Savannah: A Visual Journey Through Hampton County*. Hampton County, S.C., 2006.

McInerney, Peter. "A Call to Justice – Hampton County, South Carolina." *The University of Notre Dame Class of 1969 Blog*, 1969. notredameclassof1969blog.blogspot.com/2020/03/april-1969-call-to-justicehampton.html

McInerney, Peter. "The good, the bad, and the ugly in Hampton County." *Scholastic Magazine*, May 3, 1968.

Newspaper article archives from *The State, The Post and Courier, Greenville News, Associated Press, The Sumter Daily Item, The Columbia Record, The Press & Standard, The Beaufort Gazette, The Island Packet, The Charlotte Observer, The Atlanta Journal-Constitution, The Miami Herald*, and other newspapers around the Southeast.

The Hampton County Guardian archives, 1879-Present.

The Hampton County Tricentennial Commission. *Both Sides of the Swamp: Hampton County*. The Hampton County Historical Society, 1970.

Williams, Rose-Marie Eltzroth. *Railroads and Sawmills: Varnville, S.C. 1872 – 1997; The Making of a Low Country Town in the New South*. The Varnville Community Council, 1998.

INDEX

About the Author

Hampton County native Michael M. DeWitt Jr. is an award-winning journalist and editor of *The Hampton County Guardian*. He authored two previous history books: *Images of America — Hampton County* (2015) and *Wicked Hampton County* (2023), both published by Arcadia Publishing/The History Press. His boots-on-the-ground coverage of the Murdaugh crime saga has been published in print and online by Gannett's USA Today network. He has discussed the Murdaugh case on ABC's 20/20, CBS's 48 Hours, Dateline NBC, and Netflix documentaries.

DeWitt is the author of the Southern humor newspaper column, "Southern Voices, Southern Stories," and he has been a regular contributor for *South Carolina Wildlife* magazine and *Sporting Classics* magazine and its online counterpart *Sporting Classics Daily*.

For four years, he served as volunteer historian, storyteller and playwright for the University of South Carolina's "Salkehatchie Stew" oral history and community theater project. In 2014 he was named the Hampton County Chamber of Commerce's Person of the Year for service to the community.

Printed in the USA
CPSIA information can be obtained
at www.ICGtesting.com
CBHW051012301223
2913CB00006B/12

9 781929 647927